ARCHAEOLOGICAL SURVEY OF SOUTHERN INDIA

NOTES ON
THE AMARAVATI STUPA

ARCHAEOLOGICAL SURVEY OF SOUTHERN INDIA

NOTES ON
THE AMARAVATI STUPA

BY

JAS. BURGESS, LL.D., F.R.G.S., M.R.A.S., &c.,
GOVERNMENT ARCHAEOLOGICAL SURVEYOR FOR WESTERN AND SOUTHERN INDIA.

GYAN

Published by

Gyan Publishing House
5, Ansari Road
Daryaganj, New Delhi-110002
Phone: 011-47034999, 9811692060
E-mail: books@gyanbooks.com

Distribution Network
gyanbooks.com
India, USA, Canada, UK, Australia, France

ISBN : 978-81-212-2782-7 (HB)
First Published, 1882

2nd Impression 2021

Printed at: Gyan Press, Delhi.

Notes on
The Amaravati Stupa
Author: Jas. Burgess

Archæological Survey of Southern India.

NOTES

ON THE

AMARĀVATI STUPA,

BY

JAS. BURGESS, LL.D., F.R.G.S., M.R.A.S., &c.,

GOVERNMENT ARCHÆOLOGICAL SURVEYOR FOR WESTERN AND SOUTHERN INDIA.

Printed by Order of Government.

MADRAS:

PRINTED BY E. KEYS, AT THE GOVERNMENT PRESS.

1882.

LIST OF PLATES.

AMARĀVATI STŪPA.

THE recent history of the excavations at the Amarāvati Tope may be summed up in a few sentences. In 1876 Mr. Robert Sewell, M.C.S., then at Bezwāda, obtained a grant of Rs. 1,000 to make excavations at Amarāvati, Uṇḍavalli, &c., and began work at the Tope in May 1877, which he appears to have carried on with great care and judgment, and in his Report he very correctly states that "The object to be aimed at by any person engaged in excavating these marbles should, I think, be to fix so conclusively the position of each separate stone as it lay embedded in the soil at Amarāvati, that, whether they are transported to Madras or to London, or remain exposed where they fell, those interested in the subject and possessing the requisite scientific knowledge may be able to reconstruct the original monument, at least so far as the present position of the remains may enable them to do so. The removal of some stone, by one not possessing the requisite knowledge of the scientific importance attaching to the position in which it was found, may possibly destroy for ever all chance of determining some valuable or interesting question at present doubtful."

This, if not the only point to be attended to, was a most important one, and had it been carefully kept in view, much that is now for ever lost might have been preserved. Mr. Sewell went home on sick leave in 1879.

His Grace the Duke of Buckingham and Chandos paid a visit to the place, and on 1st February 1880, without waiting for the sanction of the expense by the Government of India, the Collector was "directed to complete at once the excavation of the Amarāvati Tope," and "authorized to expend on the work a sum of Rs. 1,000." "The Collector himself" was further ordered to "give his attention to the work, which he will be enabled to do when taking the Jamabandi of the tāluk." He was promised the assistance of a Public Works Engineer Officer, but such assistance was never sent, and he had the whole of the work, besides his onerous official duties, to attend to himself. A native was afterwards sent up to make a survey, and he made a plan which can only be interpreted on the spot and is inaccurate in important details. He also painted numbers on the stones with pitch and with no regard to inscription or carving.

The application for the Rs. 1,000 was sent to the Government of India on 24th February, when the work was nearly finished, and the reply was that it was "undesirable to make any further grant for Amarāvati while the larger question of an Archæological Survey is still pending," when "the most convenient arrangement will be to place the work at Amarāvati under the superintendence of the officer appointed to conduct the general survey." This was, however, too late as was also Lord Hartington's despatch, in which it was pointedly remarked that "Nothing is said in the Proceedings referred to of the Collector of the Krishna's special qualifications as an archæologist for undertaking these excavations. It is obvious that even inconspicuous fragments of sculptured stones, which would seem of little consequence to any one not especially acquainted with the traditions and art of Buddhism in India, might be really of the utmost importance to an expert observer, as affording indications of the history and meaning of this deeply-interesting monument of antiquity, which is unequalled for the delicacy of its details by any of the remains of Indian architectural art. Equally necessary would be the scrupulous preservation of any coins and samples of jewelry and other similar relics which may possibly be found at the Tope when it is thoroughly explored.

"I am therefore under some anxiety to hear further from your Excellency as to the steps taken for the proper excavation and conservation of the Amarāvati Tope. If these operations are not already completed, it should be borne in mind that the work of the examination and survey of an ancient monument of such unique value should be entrusted only to some competent archæologist and scholar, with such engineering assistance as you can most conveniently place at his disposal. When an accurate record has been furnished of the result of the excavations you have ordered, it will then be necessary to determine what further steps should be taken for the preservation of these sculptures, which have excited a keen interest in Europe."

Before this had been penned the unfortunate order had been carried out and the excavations completed at once. His Grace the Governor reported that "the whole area had been cleared of earth," and of any traces that may have existed of the stūpa above the original level of the foundations.

It must be added, however, that it now appears that this once splendid monument had been destroyed perhaps more than once before, and many of the beautiful slabs must have been used even within the last 65 years to burn into lime or to repair miserable Svāmi temples and similar buildings.

The recent excavations have converted the site of the tope into a large pit, roughly circular, about 75 yards in diameter, but with extensions outside the circumference at the four cardinal points which render the area somewhat of a square with very irregular sides. The removal of all the central portion of the *débris* of the tope for ever destroys the chances of getting any idea of its size or structural arrangements, but this was probably effected in the end of the last century. The stones were numbered from the south round by west and north, but many of them have been omitted in this enumeration, for what reason is hard to say. The numbers have been put on with tar and are daubed over prominent parts of the stones, sometimes across inscriptions, rendering it impossible to get a *fac-simile* owing to the thickness of the pitch, and sometimes over delicate carving, and so effectually preventing the possibility of taking a clear photograph.

The sides of the pit laid bare by the excavations present certain points that may be noted. The heights or depths of the cutting are very various in different parts, partly owing to the outturn of earth on the occasions of the different excavations having been laid up on one side or another.

Opposite to the south entrance the excavation has been carried back some way, and there we find first a stratum, consisting apparently of bricks embedded in a compact layer of clay and gravel with pieces of black pottery intermixed. Over this is a layer of 18 inches to 2 feet of broken bricks thrown together in the utmost confusion, as if washed down by a flood; over this again is a layer, varying from 4 inches to 18 inches of *kankar*, on the surface of which is a thin layer of marble chips. Evidently at the early period this indicates, the tope was either reconstructed, or, more probably, many of the marbles were utilized for other purposes. Over this is another deposit of reddish earth 8 or 10 inches deep, and then a thin layer of fragments of bricks again, the *débris* of ruined houses. This is capped at this point of the circle by a thick bed of earth with yellowish calcareous gravel or *kankar* in it.

Immediately to the west of the south entrance the stratum of broken bricks disappears, but reappears again behind the stone No. 14 (Plate I). The upper and thinner stratum also disappears, but the section presents three distinct strata—first a very compact one under the lower bricks; secondly, a redder and softer one containing occasional chips of marble above; and, thirdly, the upper one of varying thickness and containing small fragments of brick, stone, &c., which comes above the upper bricks at the gateway.

Behind Nos. 17 to 27 the marble chips strike down from the end of the layer of bricks and continue at a lower level to No. 40, and then slightly ascend again among fragments of brick. From Nos. 40 to 79 the number of discs from the rail, all with curvilinear plain backs, shows that a great destruction must have taken place here at one time, when all these smaller stones were thrown aside and the uprights which they connected carried off.

Behind No. 59 the layer of bricks thrown down anyhow commences again and gains a maximum depth of about 4½ feet near No. 80. Immediately beyond this is a layer of about 3 feet thick, also of brick pounded to pieces, and above it are some fragments of marble embedded in the bank.

Behind No. 83 the depth of the excavation again shows us the earliest stratum of bricks below, embedded in a firm clay overlaid by about 15 inches of dark reddish mould and 4 inches of gravelly soil, on which stands the foundation of a building, with plaster still adhering to the fourth, fifth, and sixth layers of bricks. Above is brick broken into small pieces and earth.

Behind the brick foundation at the west gate the bank presents only a deep layer of fine earth overlaid by others containing much of the gravelly kankar found everywhere hereabouts. At this point there seems to have been a brick dāgaba, of which only a fragment is left. It has been built of very large bricks.

Opposite No. 115 more pounded brick appears in the cutting. No. 117 lies against a small dāgaba built of small bricks, from which I obtained a small *chatti* (broken however) and a quantity of calcined bones. The foundation of a still smaller brick dāgaba is found behind stone No. 19, but it had been dug out during the late excavations and the chatti sent to the Madras Museum.

Behind No. 120 the close firm soil, apparently stratified, looks as if laid down by some great flood. Over it is broken bricks intermixed with nodules of kankar or lime; and 5 feet higher is a thin layer of bricks, which becomes deeper behind No. 141.

Behind Nos. 145 to 150 there has evidently been much brick building at different dates. At Nos.

No. 1 (Slab No. 3)

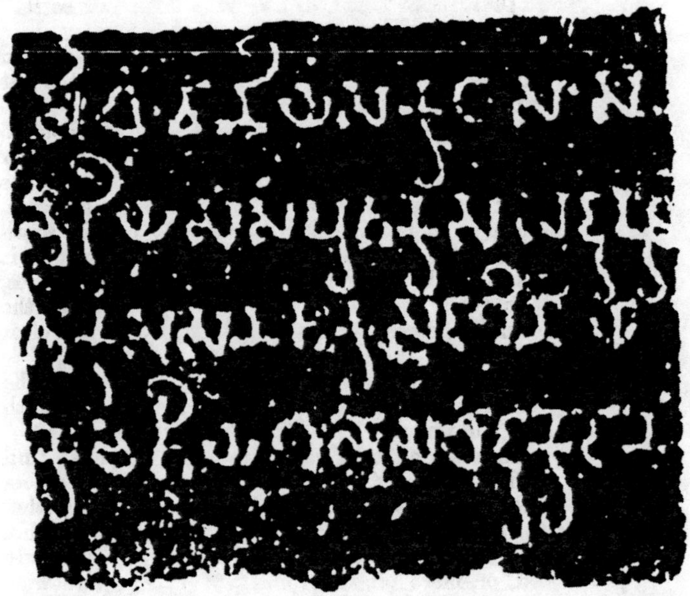

No. 2 (Slab No. 8)

No. 3 (Slab 2B)

No. 4 (Slab No. 11B)

147 to 150 the lower part of the excavation still shows bricks in layers, and the end of a wall crops out to the right of No. 157.

Opposite the north gate bricks appear low down in the cutting embedded in fine earth.

Behind No. 178, about 2 feet up, there is an old surface line with marble chips on it, then a thick layer of tumbled bricks, which continues round to nearly opposite No. 180, capped by a wavy surface line, above which is another layer of earth, then bricks again. Opposite Nos. 180 to 186 the lowest stratum of fine soft earth is well defined; then comes a thin old surface layer of firmer consistence, on which are seen chips of marble, and then a deep layer, chiefly of broken brick; but behind No. 182, above this, are more marble chips, surmounted by a deep layer of earth with brick in it.

Opposite No. 202 the lower brick layer ascends and has below it a bed of kankar. Just behind No. 205 a deep cutting has been made at no very distant date down to the level of the bottom of the pit, and marble chips, pottery and brick are distributed through nearly the whole depth. This may have extended for about 6 yards, and beyond it at least three different layers of brick, separated by others of earth, are marked. Behind No. 207 marble chips appear low in the strata and run on to No. 230, where the fall of the upper part of the embankment hides them. Considerably above them is an old surface line very straight which runs on to the south gate; above it is earth of varying depth from 2 or 3 inches to 2 feet; then broken brick; then a foot or two of earth again, and then bricks with 3 or 4 feet of earth still above them. This lower surface line looks like the result of a great flood, which possibly first destroyed, or at least greatly injured, the *stūpa*, and possibly drowned many of its priests and worshippers and led to its first falling into rapid decay.

After some violent destruction the *stūpa* seems to have been reconstructed in a rough way. The outer rail was then supported by broken pillars, images, &c. thrown in at the back of the base, and between it and a circle of dark slate slabs set on edge at about 18 inches outside the base.

At the same or a still later date the front of the bases, both of the inner and outer rail, were protected by a low breastwork of brick and plaster. It was perhaps also at the same date that the brick buildings on the platform were constructed and the images of Buddha defaced. If so, the use of lime may mark a comparatively late date.

DETAILED DESCRIPTION OF THE STONES.

As already remarked, the stones are not all numbered, nor are they all marked on the plan. To avoid further confusion the numbers on the stones are here followed, and a second series, marked B, is interspersed to designate others requiring notice.

No. 1.

No. 1, opposite the south entrance, is evidently not *in situ*. It is a slab 2 feet 7 inches broad, 3 feet high by 7 inches thick, carved on one side with a flower vase; the upper part, however, is broken off, and what is left is broken across a little below the middle. Slabs of this sort are numerous, and several of them, like this, want the marginal fillet on one side: this one wants the left border.

Nos. 22, 80, 104, 117, 129 and 130, 211, 232, 237 and 252 are slabs of the same description.

No. 2.

This is one of the cross-bars of the rail, with a circular disc 2 feet 2½ inches in diameter, the central prominence of which, as in the majority of cases, has been broken off. The back is curved and the slab set on end; it measures about 2 feet 9 inches in length, 2 feet 5 inches broad, and in the centre 7½ inches thick. It is one of the plainer pattern, carved with three circles of leaves round the centre, the first and third having a fillet of beads round them. The stone is cracked and slightly damaged along one edge.

No. 3.

At the left side of the south entrance is a portion of a pillar about 4 feet 3 inches in height, 1 foot 1½ inches broad, and 11 inches thick. It appears to have been dug out and replaced, but not precisely

2

in the position in which it was found. On the base of it (north side) is a well-cut inscription in four lines, in characters of about the first century B.C. (see Plate II, No. 1). It has been read and translated by Dr. Hultzsch of Vienna, thus :—

Sidhaṁ Vaniyasa Kuṭasa sa-
bheriyasa saputakasa saduhu-
tukasa sanatukasa dakhināyā-
ke chetiyagabho[1] *sadhāduko dānaṁ.*

Translation.—Success ! A *Chaityagarbha* containing a relic (*situated*) on the southern side, the gift of the merchant Kuṭa, together with his wife, with his sons, with his daughters, with his grandsons.

Above this in *basso rilievo* is a dāgaba 23 inches high inclusive of the numerous *chhatris* that spring like lotuses out of the capital. On the left side of the dome is a circle or star which was surmounted by some small figure (perhaps a lion), and on the right was some other figure, now broken off. (Compare the dāgaba in the Gautamīputra cave at Nāsik, *Cave Temples*, pl. xxi, fig. 2.) Above is a narrow belt 2 inches broad with a *makara* and flower ornament ; and on this stands a semi-circular ornament, or a sort of half boss, over which the corners of the pillar have been chamfered off. (Plate VIII*b*.)

On the right (west) side is a pipal tree 16 inches high, rising out of a railed enclosure or pedestal which stands on two feet of flower-vase pattern, and between which are the *Buddhapāda* or Buddha's foot-prints. Above the tree is the narrow flower band and over it the half boss. (Plate IX*a*.)

On the south face is a *chaitya* covered by a dome, and inside it is seen a dāgaba on a square base and surmounted by an umbrella. The whole is represented in bad perspective, but the sculpture is interesting as a rude picture of what was probably common in the early centuries of our era,—a dāgaba enclosed under a pillared dome or small temple with sufficient area round the central altar for circumambulation by the village Buddhists. The upper part of this side has been finished as the others, but is more injured. (Plate IX*b*.)

On the remaining (east) side is the *Dharmachakra*, standing on a pedestal similar to that below the tree, also with the *pāda* below it, and on a boss in the middle is a curvilinear *Swastika* 卐. On each side of the base of the wheel springs a rose or other flower, above which are two small circular medallions, and above the wheel, on each side, is another somewhat larger rosette with eight petals. All the carving on this pillar is in low relief and of more archaic type than the majority of the sculptures. (Plate VIII*a*.)

No. 1B (in two pieces).

This lies just to the west of No. 3 and is a broken fragment of coping (extreme dimensions 2 feet 10 inches by 1 foot 8 inches by 6 inches), but sculptured in a style that well deserves remark. Unfortunately the central figures, and indeed by far the larger part of the scene, have been ruthlessly destroyed. Built in with other broken fragments beside No. 4, I found another nearly as large portion forming the lower part of this. What is left on the two fragments consists of part of a building or gateway in the left corner and seven heads in the upper fragment with parts of two or three others. The bodies of three in front and two other figures appear in the second or lower piece. They are sculptured with a minuteness and detail that at once suggests that they are portraits. The lowest, to the left, is that of a young female with a pleasant face and pendant ear-lobes borne down by heavy ear jewels. She wears a full robe down to her ankles and is bringing in some vessel in her arms. The hair is parted in the middle with a central lock drawn back. The next figure to the right has the right hand laid across the breast, supporting some object on the forearm and with a very heavy bracelet ; the ears are pendant with a heavy ring in each ; a sort of turban encircles the head and two thick necklaces encompass the neck. Behind him is a third figure bearing a dish or present in his or her left hand, the hair enclosed in a sort of net or cap. In front of both these is another figure with full robe to the ankles, bearing some long and heavy object on the left shoulder. The next figure, above and to the right of the third, wears a turban or head-dress similar to the second, falling down over his right ear. He has also pendant ear-lobes with heavy rings in them. In front of him is a fifth, and evidently more important male personage, with enormous appendages dragging down his ears and several necklaces across his breast, while a large knob is placed on the front of his turban. He looks down to his proper left at something now broken away. To the right of this, above, is the figure of some old person with the wrinkles of age strongly marked on the now injured face ;

[1] I read this word *Chetiyakhabho*—'a Chaitya-pillar.'—J.B.

the body seems to be clothed in a full robe, the right hand lying over his waist. The head is encompassed in folds of cloth, one fold passing under the chin. In front of the left shoulder of this figure another head with a high prominence on the turban appears, but the features are destroyed. He is seated just in front of the tall male figure, at whose feet is a figure with a full *langoṭi* about his loins, lifting up his hands apparently to the seated figure. To the right was another seated on a cushion with his back to the spectator. The next figure at the top of the panel, to the right, is clad in a tunic, and apparently carries some object before him like the second. In front of his left arm is a *chauri*, held probably by the next figure, whose face, &c., has been quite destroyed.

No. 4.

Between Nos. 3 and 4 was a sort of wall made of rough lumps of marble and earth piled together, anyhow, about 14 inches thick. This I removed and found several fine fragments in it, among others, part of Nos. 1B and 81B. In front of the south edge of No. 4 stand fragments of what appear to have been two pillars, very much injured since the recent excavation. Each measures 1 foot 2 inches by 10 inches, and they are 4½ inches apart, standing face to face. No sculpture is left on either.

The back of No. 4 has been split off long ago, and only part of a line of animals is left on the inner side of what has been the first upright of the outer rail. It is 2 feet 10 inches broad and 1 foot thick, and carved on the south edge. On the back, above a fillet carved with animals, is about two-thirds of an elaborately carved disc. A chip or flaw in the stone, however, has led the workman to slope it off at the left side to fully half the height. Above the boss the corners have been filled in with rich florid designs, and the next section is divided into three shallow flutes, in which were perhaps *gaṇa* ; but in excavating, or since, the upper portion has been pounded to atoms.

No. 5.

The next stone is also as nearly as possible *in situ*. It is the lowest bar of the rail, 3 feet 9 inches long, 3 feet broad, and 1 foot thick, with a boss on the outer side 2 feet 11¼ inches in diameter, having several flaws in it. The inner side has a still richer disc on it, but has been much injured at the top by the excavators, or since.

No. 6.

Is a fragment of an upright, also *in situ*. It is 2 feet 6½ inches broad, but the inner side has been split off and destroyed, only a portion of the line of animals (see Plate XVI*b*) being left. On the back the bar of the return rail fits into it, and the remainder is carved with a circular pattern and lines of flowers below. The north edge has also been carved with a circular disc at the bottom.

No. 7.

This is the first disc of the return of the rail facing north and south, and is still *in situ*. The boss is 3 feet in diameter and 1 foot 2 inches thick, and has been beautifully carved, but, like the others, has been mercilessly pounded before and since the recent excavations. The outside disc is also well carved, the outer circle of leaves sloping back. Of the upright that extended to the corner only a few inches is left in the ground ; the rest is broken to atoms.

Nearly the same is the case with the upright (wrongly marked No. 7 on the plan) that abutted against the face of it and formed the first in the next return of the wall leading into the great circle. The fragment that remains of it shows that it was an exceptionally fine one. The lowest band has three mythological animals of the *siṁha* and *śârdûla* type between two *makaras*. In the central medallion of the half disc is a five-headed *nâga*, and the outer circle consisted of a vine (or other creeper) pattern growing out of vases at each side (see plate).

No. 8.

Behind the stone to the west of No. 7 lies a thin pillar 1 foot 4½ inches by 9½ inches, and about 4 feet 2 inches high ; it has had the usual semi-circular ornament above and below on all sides, with the edges chamfered off between. The semi-circles are only 11 inches apart, and the pillar was originally probably not very much longer than it still is. On the one side of it is an inscription in 10½ lines, letters small and much injured (see Plate II, No. 2). It commenced :—

Sidhaṁ Namo Bhagavato, &c.

No. 9.

This stands between No. 8 and 1B, and is probably not far from where it was found, though at what level is uncertain. It is the corner of a piece of coping, badly broken at the left end; is 3 feet 3 inches long at the top, but much less below, 2 feet 7½ inches high, and 8 inches thick, having apparently been split, possibly off No. 1B.

It is carved with a large *gaṇa* at the right end, with a gruesome face, holding the end of the large roll, that winds up and down along all these coping stones, as if he were pulling it all out of his mouth. On the lower bight just in front of him is a medallion with a double border enclosing a dāgaba with a worshipper on each side of it. Above this is a throne with cushions, from the back of which rises a short pillar surmounted by the *dharmachakra*, or 'Wheel of the Law,' and also with a worshipper on each side. The upward turn of the roll is supported by a human figure with large heavy rings in his ears and a large turban with the prominence in front so frequent in figures of the Andhra period. In the next space, above the roll, has been probably a dāgaba, — the umbrella and a worshipper being left. Below the whole is a border of leaves.

No. 2B.

This stone, lying partly behind No. 10 (it is wrongly marked No. 9 on the plan), is another piece of coping, and must have been at a corner. It is not cut in such relief as the last, but with remarkable detail, though much mutilated. Its extreme length is 5 feet 9 inches, 2 feet 2 inches high, and 7¼ inches thick, being also split. The end has been carved with some sort of winged lion. The right end begins with a large *makara*, from the mouth of which a female, with three very heavy anklets, unusually large breasts and eyes, striped drawers, and a star or rose on her forehead, is pulling out the long roll which fills the area. The space over the first bend is filled with a semi-circle much in the style of those at the tops and bottoms of pilasters. The upward bend is supported by a *gaṇa*, with large features, moustache, wrinkled brow, and a close fitting cap with two tails sticking out of it; his head is turned clean over his shoulder. There is a band of rosettes below, and a leaf-and-bell flower pattern above. On the rounded top is part of an inscription: the left-hand portion is broken away and what is left reads :—

. . . [*sa duhu*]*tukāyasa natukāya unisa*[1] *dānaṁ*

Dr. Hultzsch reads this as : "An *Ushṇīsha* (?) the gift of . . . [*with her daughters*] with her grandsons." (See Plate II, No. 3.)

Behind Nos. 10 and 11 lies the other half of the last, but it is quite plain on the back.

No. 10.

We now return to the stones *in situ* on the left side of the entrance court. Next to the fragment of the base of an upright already described is a disc of the rail, which, like all the neighbouring stones here, has suffered severely by pounding with stones since the excavation. It is 2 feet 10½ inches in diameter by 1 foot 4¾ inches thick, with a double row of leaves round the outer border. At the bottom of the area are a number of water plants and three birds. In the centre sits a Buddha on a throne, his knees at the ends of the seat and his feet on a stool. The representation is unusually awkward. On his right sits a *Nāgarāja*, his feet on some rich footstool and his hands raised in worship. On the other side is his queen in a similar attitude, while behind the *Nāgarāja* is another *Nāganī* squatted and worshipping. Behind her is a third, and behind the throne and to the left of it are four people, one of them at least a male. To the right, behind the first *Nāganī*, is a standing female, perhaps a *chauri*-bearer, and between her and Buddha's head are three other heads; behind her also is another standing female. These two females are dressed exactly as the figures on the screen walls at Kārle and Kaṇheri. The upper part of the area

---

[1] This word, elsewhere spelt *uṁtisa*, means a coping stone.

is very much destroyed, almost all the figures being split off. It evidently represented a scene in the clouds, with the *Devas* (and, perhaps, a horse among them) all listening to the Buddha's teaching.

The back of the stone is a carved disc.

No. 11.

This is the base of the next pillar in the rail, and it has suffered above like the rest. The stone, however, was partially decayed. It is 2 feet 10½ inches wide by 13 inches thick, probably split to the bottom, and has two-thirds of a disc over a string of animals on the inner side, and the greater part of a similar carving in better preservation on the back. (See Plate XVI*h*.)

No. 12.

This is another disc; the upper half of the inner side entirely gone. What remains shows four people, with the high Andhra turbans, sitting on richly carved stools, and a fifth behind to the left, while the leg of a sixth figure higher up to the right comes down over the seat and touches the head of one of the figures below. This has been separated from another scene on the right by a pillar. Apparently it contained a rider on horseback with two little figures below. The rest is entirely destroyed.

The back of the slab has a well carved disc.

No. 13.

This is one of a large number of discs set down on end and out of position. It is 3 feet 10 inches in diameter and 13 inches thick, well carved on one side, but a part of the back split off.

No. 3B.

Just in front of this lies a fragment of what must have been an elaborate carving of a pipal or *bodhi* tree, with an umbrella over it and attendants.

No. 14.

This beautiful disc has fortunately escaped much damage, except to the flanges and back. It had been lying with the face down and so has been preserved. It is almost impossible to describe the scene. A platter bearing a bowl is held up by a circle of fourteen dancing figures, and round these dance in frantic style two other concentric circles containing 33 or 34 figures, of which about a third only, and these in the upper part of the area, are females, some of them bearing what may be presents. The head dresses vary, but the Andhra style with the high knob in front predominates. A similar scene is figured from a drawing in Mr. Fergusson's *Tree and Serpent Worship*, plate lxxiii, fig. 2, and a portion of another on plate lxvii.

No. 4B.

Just in front of this I found a large fragment of a coping stone, 2 feet 9 inches by 2 feet 5 inches, lying on its face.

On the left are three figures in the dress of *Bhikshus* coming in at a gate. Outside it is a very tall figure, seizing with his left hand a man on the neck of an elephant which has gone down on his hind knees; the tall man has his left foot on its shoulder, while with his right hand he holds a club or sword. Between him and the gate are other two men. Over his head a figure kneels to the *Buddhapāda* with the pillar of flame springing from them, surmounted by the *triśūla;* behind is another figure, and over the gate is a second warrior with his sword about to strike either the flaming pillar or its worshipper. To the right of the pillar is a tall female.

Behind No. 14 or rather No. 19 is the base of a small brick dāgaba about 3 feet in diameter: the relic casket consisting of a *chatti* found in it, was sent to Madras by the Collector two years ago.

No. 15.

This is a round disc, the purpose of which is not apparent. It is 10 inches thick, 2 feet 11 inches diameter at the back, which is quite flat, and 2 feet 9 inches in front; and as it never seems to have had any flanges it may have formed a finial.

No. 16.

This is a fragment 2 feet 9 inches by 1 foot 7 inches, and 5 inches thick, carved with three *triśūla* symbols (one of them broken). There are still iron plugs in the centres of the two that are entire. Below is a wavy florid border.

No. 17.

This is a disc richly carved and set down on end; the back is much injured. It is 2 feet 9½ inches in diameter.

No. 18.

This stands near the corner where the outer rail returned into the circle, and is carved with two *triśūlas* having iron pins in their centres. It is only a fragment, 1 foot 9 inches high by 1 foot 10 inches broad, and about 5 inches thick, with rough back.

No. 19.

This has been a very fine disc *in situ*, but much pounded and injured during or since excavating.

No. 20.

The base of a pillar smashed similarly to so many others. In this case it would appear that the pillar was tolerably entire before the recent excavations; for beside it lies a fragment of the edge 2 feet 6 inches in length, carrying it up from the level of the top of the lower semi-circle to near the middle of the central one, with four human figures on the 8 inches of the face which it preserves.

Nos. 5B and 6B.

Are two fragments, one 3 feet 3 inches long, by about 8 inches broad, and the other a corner 1 foot long, forming the bottom of a thin slab, with numerous figures, of which we have only portions left.

No. 21.

This again is a fine disc *in situ* between Nos. 20 and 24. It has been pounded with stones which have been brought down on it with no tender hand, cutting off also the upper corners of the flanges, the places where inscriptions are frequently to be found. The back is perfect.

No. 22.

A fragment of a flower vase 4 feet 11 inches in height and 1 foot 9 inches at broadest. It has had no margin at the left side, but an inscription at the bottom in two lines of which only a fragment is left—

(Si)dhaṁ Mugudāsanaputasa maramupa . . . .
. . . *putukā . sasu . kaṁ nasana(ta ?)* . . . .

No. 23.

A disc lying buried in the ground behind No. 24 (possibly like No. 15).

No. 24.

A large fragment of a pillar 3 feet 1½ inches broad and standing about 5 feet 9 inches out of the ground. It has been savagely hammered atop and down the edges, and is broken across the middle. The lowest portion of the carving is a band of animals; on the left a *makara* gaping after a sort of lion with horns; and on the right a similar *makara* pursuing a tiger; in the centre is a flower; and the interspaces are carved with leaves. Above this is fully half a circle carved in concentric circles of leaves like the discs. The corners over this are filled with foliage to the line of the top of the circle, and the space between this line and the bottom of the next medallion is divided into three panels filled with human figures. The left one has been badly damaged since the recent excavations. In the right of it is a door at which stands a child, while a woman is rushing excitedly in, looking back at something now broken away. Just behind her is another with her back to the spectator and her hand raised to her face. In front, to the left, a woman lies or has fallen, but partly rests against another who sits on her knees. Behind these has been a fourth with her back to the spectator. Above is left the head and arm of a figure, perhaps flying, who seems to be threatening those below.

In the central compartment are a dozen figures, the central one a tall male stretching up his left hand to the top of the panel, while in his right, held off from his side, he has a short sword pointing downwards. All the others seem to be females and children in a state of the greatest alarm at this threatening figure. In the lower right corner is a child on whose head the mother, stooping on one knee, lays her right hand, while she looks back at the threatening man. Against her back falls a younger woman; against her a third, who leans her hand on the shoulder of the first. Above the man's outstretched arm is a face—bent to one side as if in pain or grief. On the other side, behind the sword, is a child on its mother's knee, who crouches in the corner. Beyond his arm is another mother rushing off with her child, and behind her are two other females. In the upper corners of the panel are two pear (or balloon) shaped trees. The stories in these compartments are vividly told, and may, perhaps, be identified among the Buddhist legends.

The third or right side compartment seems to belong to the same story. The central figure is a male standing or dancing on the back of a fallen figure, both his arms thrown up, swinging an infant by the leg in each hand. On each side stands on tiptoe another male figure, that to the right having a battle-axe. The corners, under what has been the central medallion, are filled with foliage. The central disc had a florid border round it, and below a floor on which the figures sit or stand. But here, again, another very interesting scene has been ruined,—apparently quite recently.

What is left of this may be described as follows: In the centre has sat a rāja on a *siṁhasana* or lion-throne, his left foot doubled up before him and the right on a footstool. On each side sat other figures. In front, on the floor, sit four men. The one in front of the footstool has his left arm round his neighbour's neck, as if constraining him to some action: he points with his right hand to the scene to the right. The other two figures to the left are in the act of supplicating the throne. To the right a figure stands with his arms akimbo, while a man standing up pulls him back by the right arm, and another, kneeling, holds him by the right leg, as if to restrain him from leaving. The head of this figure is gone with all the other portions of what must have been an animated scene. The back of this pillar is probably buried in the earth. The half disc below is separated, as in front, from the central disc by a space divided into three panels, with three dancing *gaṇa*, one in each compartment, but one of them is much broken. The central disc is all shattered as if pounded with stones.

No. 25.

Beside the last, and probably belonging to it, is a disc or boss 2 feet 10 inches diameter, well carved in front but damaged on the back.

Nos. 7B and 8B.

In front of a small brick foundation on the procession path lies a pillar apparently of the inner rail, 8 feet 2 inches by 1 foot 6½ inches by 10½ inches, with mortises for four bars on each side. It has, at a later date, been used for some other purpose, as the carving, consisting of a central disc and an upper and lower half disc, is covered over with lime. The back is plain. It has been cracked through in laying it down where it is. There is a mark on the edge of it.

Near by lies a lenticular bar 1 foot 10½ inches long, 1 foot 6½ inches broad, which must also have belonged to this rail. It is perfectly plain on both sides, and others, like it, lie about elsewhere.

No. 9B.

This is in a very different style of carving from most of the others, being in low relief. It is 2 feet 6 inches by 11½ inches, and of variable thickness. Above a quadrantal moulding is a narrow plain facia with four upright oblong holes in it. Over this is a narrow curved belt that has been carved with animals after the style of some of the Nāsik friezes. Above this is a frieze 6½ inches broad, the right half of it carved with rail pattern; three uprights with two cross-bars between. The uprights have half discs above and below, and three flutes connecting them. On one cross-bar is a figure beating a drum; on the one below it is a rosette; on the other two are a rosette and elephant; to the right of the third upright is a pipal tree. At the left end of the stone is a single upright, and the space to the right of it is carved with five dancing figures, the central one bearing a tray on his head. This probably belongs to an early date in the history of the Stūpa.

No. 10B.

This is a fragment 2 feet 10 inches long, 9½ inches high, and 4½ inches thick, and is carved with three dāgabas and as many Buddhas in alternation, separated by narrow pilasters in the background.

No. 11B.

A similar piece 1 foot 9 inches by 9 inches by 6 inches, containing two dāgabas and part of a third with Buddhas between. On the top of this is a lense-shaped hole, as if it had once been used for an upright. The dāgabas are narrower than in the last, and the compartments are not divided off in the same way, so that they are not parts of the same band. Below this is part of an inscription not easily made out from the lime filling in the letters, which were only faintly carved at first. (See Plate II, No. 4.) It appears to read—

-vasikāsa mahākhā (?) *najakāsa bhāyatā* (?) *nādhasirisasise..yachā* (?) *bu* .....

No. 12B.

This is a very similar piece, and may have formed part of the same course. It is 2 feet 2 inches by 9½ inches by 3½ inches, and has three dāgabas with two intervening Buddhas. It has likewise an inscription below in one line, which, so far as I can make it out, reads—

Sidhaṁ Namo Bhagavato savasatutamasa Budhasa Maṁdaravāthavasa pava ta siuṁtasa bhaginiya ...

Dr. Hultzsch renders this—"Success! Adoration to the holy Buddha the best of all beings! [The gift of ...] the sister of the ascetic Siuṁtā (Śrigupta) who resides at Maṁdara. (See Plate III, No. 5.)

No. 13B.

This piece, 2 feet 8 inches by 8½ inches, by about 6½ inches, is much damaged: it has also been built in with lime into some structure. At the left end is a Buddha on a throne with two *chauri*-bearers and some worshippers. In the middle is a rāja perhaps seated, with four attendants to the left above, one of them a *chauri*-bearer, and a suppliant below. A figure appears under the throne to the right; then a standing figure, apparently carrying a bar; beside him is another figure; behind the throne a second *chauri*-bearer; and above, one apparently flying through the air. Still to the right is another figure on a throne, with his feet on a stool, his hands crossed on his breast, and two *chauri*-bearers behind the throne. To the left below is a seated figure addressing him, and above a figure squatted Buddha fashion. On the right below is a *Nāgarāja* and his wife, seated in reverential attitude; and above another male and female. To the right of all is a dāgaba. This stone has a mortise-hole in the upper edge.

No. 14B.

This measures 3 feet 6 inches by 8½ inches by 6 inches, and has three large mortises in the lower edge. The sculpture is in three compartments. First on the left is an object resembling a dāgaba with a tree on each side, but no umbrella. The surface too is carved in a rude chequer, not met with elsewhere, and it is possible it may represent a hut in the forest. To the right of it stands a man with a child on his neck and a woman with another on her shoulder. To the right two people are meeting and taking each other by the hands, while a third, apparently a female, with hands joined, appears behind; these are followed by a covered cart in very bad perspective, and in the background are trees.

A pillar or wall on each side the next compartment marks an in-door scene. A great man sits on his throne; two *chauri*-bearers stand behind it, and two people, probably male and female, come in from the left and address him with uplifted hands. Behind them are two spectators.

In the third panel an elephant enters from the right, his head and forelegs only being shown. A man apparently lays some object on a pedestal, the foot of which is in the form of a dwarf; another stands behind with perhaps a *chauri*, and five others to the left look on.

No. 5 (Slab No. 12 B)

No. 6 (Slab No. 49 B)

No. 9 (Slab No. 86)

No. 7 (Slab No. 54)

No. 8 (Slab No. 80)

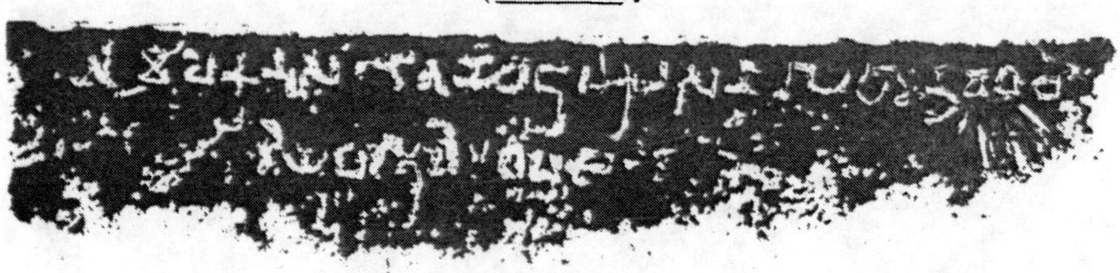

J. Burgess fecit

No. 15B.

Laid down on the verge of the inner circle in a line, and their position marked on the plan but not numbered, are nine small stones, which, from the lime upon them, must have been built into some structure.

The first is a small stone 2 feet 8 inches long by about 5 inches square, probably broken at the both ends. It is sculptured similarly to the uppermost line on the large slab from Masulipatam and other dāgaba slabs. At the left end are a standing male and female, being part of a panel otherwise destroyed. Three carved buttons divide these from the next, in which is a seated Buddha with a worshipper on each side, that to the right destroyed. Then three more knobs and a male and female, the former holding the latter by the hand, while she seems to wish to part from him. Three knobs again divide off the scene, and to the right of the uppermost are two bullocks' heads with long horns; then a female addressing Buddha, who sits on a throne with three vessels before it, and to his right are two female suppliants. Again come a male and female, separated by the usual knobs from the other scenes; and, lastly, a figure seated on a throne—not as a Buddha—with a horse eating beside him and a figure holding up a cloth to the left; another is behind him, and above a *Dēva* or *Gandharva*. There has also been one to the right, but it is broken here. It is a pity this stone is so injured.

No. 16B.

A small fragment, probably of a flower vase slab, with portions of two lines of inscription upon it apparently reading—

-sidhathasa thariyāya bhagoṁ magha
bodhiya vadataṁ imada dhama.

No. 17B.

Is a small fragment, about 8 inches by 9 inches, with three Buddha's heads and two lotus flowers above.

No. 18B.

This was set against the brick-work in front of No. 29, and is 1 foot 4 inches high and 7 inches broad. It has a standing figure of Buddha, with an attendant on a support upheld by one or more figures, but is much encrusted with plaster.

No. 19B. & 20B.

The larger fragment, with a fillet of animals and plants along the bottom; on the right a figure on horseback—heads of both gone—and another behind under a tree. To the left is the lower part of a standing Buddha.

The smaller fragment may possibly be another piece of the same slab.

No. 21B.

This is a round block with a deep hole in the centre.

No. 22B.

On the inner edge of the platform I dug up three portions of a narrow pilaster. It had been thrown down behind the inner parapet on the platform and apparently broken in the fall. The lower of the three panels left is divided into two. On the left a man and woman are seated, and the man puts his finger on her temple or over the eye, while she seems to steady her head with her hands. Below is a figure with a long sword. On the right is Buddha preaching and a man with high head-dress is presenting an alms-bowl to him. In the next panel above is Buddha preaching on his throne—the Bodhi tree showing on each side the nimbus. Below is a man seated with a high peak on his turban, and another figure with a cloth over the head and shoulders, kneeling in worship. At the sides are six other figures.

The third panel seemingly represents a king in his harem with a wife seated beside him and food placed at his feet. He has a high flat-topped hat and seven ladies appear around. It may be noted that in all these sculptures, the females when in presence of a rāja, are always represented as nude to the waist. This indicates an early and perhaps universal custom in India, of females baring their breast in token of respect when in presence of any royal personage. In the upper left corner of this panel is Buddha and a disciple apparently moralizing.

Of the fourth panel. above this, only a corner is left.

No. 23B.

This is a very curious palimpsest slab. Originally it has been part of one of the dāgaba slabs, of which most fortunately Sir W. Elliot recovered several. The only others now left perhaps being the very fine one from Masulipatam, and a broken one, No. 53, here described in its place, one fragment, No. 253, and another with the snake on it, now worshipped at the east end of the village.

This is 3 feet 7 inches long, 1 foot 3¼ inches high, and about 4 inches thick, and has lost a piece at the left upper corner. It is divided into three unequal panels. In the smallest, on the right, are only a man and woman; he holds some object over her head, and she holds a string which passes through his girdle.

In the second panel a prince sits upon his throne; two women sit on a seat to the left, both apparently asleep; two others are in the same condition on the right; two lie below to the left; another nods over her *sittar*, and two more to the right over their drums. A very marked face, apparently an older female, looks in to the right of him and two more to the left. This is a well-known scene, that of the night of Gautama departure from Kapilavastu.

The next naturally follows. In the middle Gautama or Siddhārtha is mounted on his horse; *gana* bear up its feet; a man behind carries the royal umbrella over the prince; at the gate out of which he has just come a man is straining with a lever to close the way. Two or three figures above carry lights, and some five dance along before the rider. Below, the whole compartment is supported by little owl-like figures with grotesque faces. (See Plate X.)

No. 24B.

Another piece broken from the left end of this stone I found at a short distance; it measures 1 foot 3 inches high by 1 foot 4 inches broad, but the sculpture on it is much defaced. In the centre is Buddha, perhaps seated, with the right leg turned up on the seat and the left foot on a small stool; from behind a horse, with bridle, comes round and looks at him from the right, and two *dêvatas* or *gandharvas* above and five human beings listen to his teaching.

No. 26.

A rail bar just behind No. 25, and has been excavated without serious injury. The front disc is 2 feet 11 inches in diameter, the bar 3 feet 5 inches in length and 1 foot 3 inches thick. The back is boldly carved in concentric circles. The front is beautifully executed. In the centre is a king on his throne with the Andhra turban and a large oval disc behind his head, marked with a chequer or tartan-like pattern. Behind are five servants, two of them at least females. A figure in the middle distance and to the right is addressing him with joined hands, another with a high head-dress and abundant clothing lays his joined hands on the arm of the throne. In front and sculptured with considerable skill are two men, one in the Andhra dress and the other a Negro with a long *angarakha* down to his ankles, and a long straight sword hanging down from his left hip to his right ankle. He holds a horse which is only partly seen on the extreme right beyond a pillar of the hall. Beyond the Negro is another figure with short-cut hair; and above the horse is an elephant with the *mahaut* resting his chin on his arms over its forehead. Below the throne is a footstool with a soft cushion on it, upon which the rāja rests his left foot, and beside it is a dwarf. Still lower are four men, apparently Negroes, in a sort of kilt dress, also with what appear to be two chased vessels, a string of pearls and a letter, which one of them applies to the footstool.

On the extreme left and lower than the rāja sits the Rānī; a female below her chafes her foot; two beyond are her *chauri*-bearers, and one, with hair crimped, stands between her and the throne. Two more above look on with apparent interest.

No. 27.

This is a similar stone to No. 26, the disc in front being 2 feet 11½ inches in diameter. In the upper central portion is a throne with cushions, from the back of which springs the flaming pillar crowned by the *triśūla.* Two *chauri*-bearers, with their hair in a peculiar top-knot, stand behind the ends of the throne; two kneel in front with their hair brought into a thick roll round their necks. Other three figures join them. On a small platform on the left stands a man, apparently coming out of a building, playing upon the *sittar* and followed by another, with a staff, apparently begging. The remaining twelve figures that fill up the area are all devotees of the yellow robe. The back of the stone is quite split off.

No. 28.

This is a beautiful boss with discs on both sides, 2 feet 11½ inches in diameter.

No. 29.

Another disc deep in the earth.

No. 30.

This is a tall upright slab, about 9 feet high, 2 feet 9 inches broad, and 11 inches thick, with mortises on each edge for four cross-bars. The whole of the lower half of the central medallion has been hewn out by some Goth, leaving a hollow across the stone about 10 inches wide and 4 inches deep. Above the string of animals, which always forms the lowest portion of the carving on such stones, is about two-thirds of a circular disc. The corners over it are filled in with foliage, and the area between them and the central disc is divided into three compartments. In that on the left is a *Nāgarāja* with his right hand uplifted as if asseverating: in front to the right is a *gaṇa*; beyond him another; and higher to the right a man with his hands joined. To the left are two figures, apparently coming out of a building, the one in front with his knuckles stuck into his sides.

In the central panel there are again two dwarfs, also in excited attitudes. A man on the left seems to be running a spear into the side of the central figure, who leans on the hand of another to the right; and a fourth figure, perhaps a female, catches the third by the upraised wrist. Another figure behind, between the first and second, has his arm raised as if to strike.

In the third compartment a man to the left holds a *sittar*; a dwarf rushes forward, with objects in both hands, and a figure to the right seems to be dancing, while there are three others in the background. The right side of this panel is broken off.

What remains of the central disc shows that it was intended to be a companion picture to that in No. 27. The flaming *triśūla* pillar on the throne is the central object, and over or behind it is a *Bodhi* tree. A *chauri*-bearer attends on each side behind the throne, and nine men, with the high Andhra turban, pay reverence on the left. On the right five above are all ladies. On the extreme right is one in ample clothing, her head wrapped closely up and with an aged face. In front of and below her is a corpulent gentleman. The rest is destroyed.

Above this again are three panels, the left one much injured, but containing a dwarf, a man with his hands joined facing to the right, and to the left of him a figure in an ample tunic.

In the middle, apparently on a flaming throne, is Buddha seated; a man and woman are below it; two men to the left, and two to the right of it.

The right side panel had four standing figures, but all are much defaced. On the back the lower three hollow compartments are filled by frolicing *gaṇa*.

In the upper three, a dāgaba, with two men worshipping it, occupies the centre; two men and a dwarf saluting it are in the right; and two men (the dwarf broken off) in the left panel.

No. 31.

The base of another rail pillar, but only parts of the lower half discs are left.

No. 32.

This is half of a rail disc, the back split off.

No. 33.

One side of a split coping stone. The flower roll is upheld by tall human figures, and at the left end is a dāgaba and worshipper; at the right a tree within a circular wall and two persons offering flower vases.

No. 34.

A somewhat worn simple disc (see No 39), the centre of it broken out, the flanges almost entire.

No. 34 *bis* (also marked No. 35).

This is an irregular fragment, about 2 feet 4 inches each way, representing the front of some building with arched windows, one above and two below, and much rail-pattern ornament; but it is much abraded. There has been an inscription above, but it is almost illegible; I read doubtfully the syllables,—

. . . . . . piya
. . . . . . gilamatuya . . . . laviya.

No. 35.

A small fragment of a similar stone, 1 foot 9 inches by 1 foot, bearing one of the *triśūla* figures.

No. 36.

This is a disc 2 feet 4 inches in diameter and somewhat peculiarly carved, perhaps older than most of the others: it is one of those, however, which have a plain rounded back. On the upper left corner is a fragment of an inscription.

yakamāyasa . .
siniya (?) dāna.

No. 37.

A piece of coping about 4 feet long by 2 feet 9 inches high; the great roll is supported by two men running to the left. On the lower bend of the roll is a medallion containing the sacred tree, with two cushions on the throne; in front of it is a worshipper on each side. In the space above is a dāgaba and two men reverencing it.

On the other side has been some very animated scenes, unfortunately, as usual, much damaged. From the left enter four riders on elephants; below is a lady on horseback; three heads, apparently of females, appear behind; another in front of the first horse is advancing towards another horse held by a small groom. Above, in a doorway, the backs of five ladies' heads are seen entering, while one stands by the jamb, as if welcoming them. The right-hand scene has had a Buddha on a throne, in front of which a box or footstool is upheld by a small figure, and six women kneel in reverence in front; to the left sits a male in Andhra attire, and behind him stands a woman and again two above and behind them, all saluting the Buddha. The figures to the right are all broken off.

No. 38.

Another piece of rail coping: a single block 2 feet 1 inch broad by 2 feet 9 inches high. On the right is a throne, with a dwarf below it, two *chauri*-bearers and another servant behind; from it the *rāja* seems just to have descended and is standing saluting four priests in long robes, who are coming out of the gate of a monastery or *stūpa* (a copy of the Sānchi gates), while between him and them a figure kneels at their feet, and in the background another figure stands with joined hands.

The other side of the stone has a well-carved scaly *makara* with a dwarf seated on his forehead.

Nos. 39, 40, and 41.

These three discs are 2 feet 2½ inches, 2 feet 2 inches, and 2 feet 4 inches in diameter, with carved backs and large tenons. They are all of the same pattern. Nos. 42, 43, 48, 51, 57, 58, 59, 60, 61, 62, 63, 64, 65, 66, 67, 68, 70, 71, 75, 76, 77, 78, and 79 appear all to have belonged to the same series, besides many broken ones lying about here. They hardly require further notice. From No. 43 about a third is broken off.

No. 44.

A large fragment of an old pillar 1 foot 11½ inches broad and about 4½ feet high by 8¾ inches thick, the lower half disc and what is left of the upper one, carved in the same early style and pattern as the rail discs just mentioned. It has, however, gone through several vicissitudes, for the back seems at one time to have been sculptured and then hewn off, and both edges are wrought into three receding facias, each 1¾ inches behind the other. Then a circular hole 9½ inches diameter has been cut through the stone just under the central disc, as if to bear the thick bar of a gate or the pillar of a chhatra; lastly, four mortise holes have been cut, two on each edge.

No. 45.

This is a fragment, 5 feet 9 inches long, about 1 foot 7 inches broad, and 6 inches thick, of a coping stone split up and much knocked about. An elephant-headed dwarf (? the original of Gaṇēsa) bears up a part of the roll. The areas above it have been filled in with half discs of the same pattern as on Nos. 39–43, &c.

No. 46.

Lying in the trench was a much worn slab, 3 feet 4 inches by 11 inches, having at the top parts of a dāgaba and two worshippers, and in the middle a tree in a small enclosure with the head of a worshipper to the left. There seem also to have been *dēvas* with presents at each side.

No. 47.

Is part of the base of a pillar similar to No. 44. It had split, however, and has been rivetted by a strong iron bolt through the centre of the piece, which measures 2 feet 11 inches by 2 feet broad and 11 inches thick; only a part of the lower half disc is left at the head of it.

No. 48.

This is a disc similar to No. 39, &c., but broken in two.

No. 49.

Is a fragment 2 feet 2 inches by 10 inches by 7 inches, which must have been part of a coping stone, but has been squared for a post, with a semicircular hollow in one end to support a bar.

No. 25B.

A fragment of the upper portion of an outer rail pillar with eight syllables of an inscription on it. (See Plate III, 6.)

No. 50.

1 foot 10½ inches by 7 inches by 7 inches. This is a nearly square pillar, one corner rounded off. In front is a dāgaba in low relief, with a small rosette to each side of the capital; the *chattras* in the second row over it have been cut away.

No 51.—See No. 39.

No. 52.

2 feet 7 inches broad and about the same high, by 4½ inches thick. The lower portion of a slab carved with uncommon care. Four female figures (one without the head) and the *Buddhapāda* which they worship, is all that is now left. Over the *pāda*, which rests on a stool, has been a throne. This slab has at one time been attached by plaster on the front to some wall or formed a step. The figures are larger than usual, and the minute details of their coiffure, which seems to form the principal part of their dress, are expressed with much care. (See Plate XI.)

No. 26B.

This is a mere fragment, 2 feet 1 inch long, of a small slab with the remains of three figures of Buddha and two dāgabas between, also some letters of an inscription below. It has at one time been part of an upright and has a groove along the back.

No. 53.

2 feet 6 inches by 4 feet 8 inches by 5 inches. This is a very fine slab, unfortunately broken across the upper left corner. The centre is occupied by a dāgaba 1 foot 4½ inches broad by 2 feet 11 inches, exclusive of the great cluster of umbrella-like flowers that crown it. On the drum are three compartments, each filled by a five-hooded snake. Three others are knotted round the dome. It would appear that the sculptor had injured the figures first carved on the right edge, for they are now on a much lower level than those on the left. Below is a female *Nāganī* offering a flower. The carving of this figure is inferior, but there is a curious Gorgon head in her head-dress. Above her is the *Nāgarāja*, holding up with his first three fingers a flower which a bee is sucking; his curls fly out at each side of the head; the head-dress is elaborate and is crowned by a grotesque face, over which rises the five hoods of the snake. Above has been another figure, now chipped off. On the left side, below, is a *Nāganī* kneeling and worshipping,—her hair combed back and held in by a simple fillet or coronet.

Above her is the rāja with the Andhra head-dress, offering a flower with his right hand (the arm has been knocked off and the snake-hood damaged), and above him is a smaller *Nāgarāja* in the air with a tray of fruit as an offering (this is on the portion broken off).

No. 54.

4 feet 9 inches by 1 foot 1½ inches by 4½ inches. This slab has been built in with lime on both edges, as has also the preceding. The left edge of the upper two compartments of the four into which it is divided had been broken off previously to this, but the upper one has been broken off by careless handling. At the top is part of an inscription in two lines, (see Plate III, No. 7) that seems to read:—

. . Bhagavato Kavururavaṭhaviya pavajato paya
. . . hagiya bhoyitiya bedhiya utaya mahadakapatitha.a

The upper panel contains a dāgaba with Buddha preaching in front, the five steles above, lions on the rail, four dēvas worshipping the top; and in a toraṇa doorway to the right is a female worshipper; the left side is gone.

The second panel (recently broken across the top) has Buddha teaching; two deer in front of the throne; three figures worshipping on the right, and originally the same on the left.

The third contains Buddha preaching, on a throne supported in front by three *gaṇa*, while three ladies on the right and two on the left with two men seem more inclined to scoff at the saint's asceticism than to receive his teaching.

In the lowest compartment the prince Siddhārtha goes away on his horse, its hoofs upheld by *gaṇa*; a man in a kilt with two spears advances in front; a regal-like personage (? Indra) holds the *chhatra*; and other three give attendance. The crowbars have left their marks on this panel.

No. 55.

About 2 feet by 2 feet. This is a large fragment from the top of a flower-vase slab.

No. 27B.

Is the upper portion of a slab similar to No. 54, but it appears to have been built in and the face is much wasted.

Behind Nos. 53 and 54 are piled up a heap of broken pieces, among them a lenticular cross-bar perfectly plain, two toes of a *pāda*, &c.

No. 56.

About 2 feet 4 inches each way. A fragment of a coping stone which has been split and built in. Over the bend of the roll is the throne with the *Dharmachakra* above, and two male figures worshipping it; on the roll below is a rosette medallion.

Nos. 57, 58, and 59.—See No. 39.

No. 60.

Is a similar disc 2 feet 3¾ inches diameter, but rather more richly carved, in that the leaves in the outer circle are rounded at the points and have a line of beads on the midrib. There has been an inscription on the upper right-hand corner on the bar, but only the letters

budhara(?)
jidu (*dā* ?)

are distinguishable.

No. 28B.

A small fragment of one of the large thin slabs with the ends of two lines of inscription.

Nos. 61, 62, 63, 64 and 65.

See No. 39. Of No. 61 the front is peeled off and No. 63 is broken.

No. 66.

This disc has had four concentric circles round the centre, the outer one filled with a creeper pattern. It is much abraded. On the upper left corner is a fragment of an inscription, which Dr. Hultzsch reads—

[Sama]*nikāya*
[Si]*dhathiyā*
deya dhama

"The meritorious gift of the female ascetic [Si]dhathí (Siddhārṭhī)."—(Dr. Hultzsch.)

No. 67.

This is half a disc, similar in pattern, but in better preservation.

No. 68.

A fine disc of the No. 39, &c., pattern.

No. 69.

About 2 feet 6 inches by 1 foot 10 inches high, and 5½ inches thick. This is a piece of split coping with a bull in full career below and a florid belt above.

Nos. 70 and 71.—See No. 39.

No. 72.

About 1 foot 9 inches broad by 4 feet 3 inches high. The left portion of a large thin slab divided into two panels, the lower containing a pipal or *bodhi* tree with a man and woman to the left making offerings in pots, and a *dēva* above with a present on a flat dish. The other side and bottom are broken off.

A fillet carved with tigers all running to the left divides this from the upper panel, on which is a throne with two cushions on it; below it the *pāduka*, and over it a short lion pillar supporting the *Dharmachakra*. To the left are two men in Andhra head-dress worshipping it; there has been a *dēva* above; the right side is broken off.

Nos. 73 and 29B.

About 2 feet by 2½ feet, and 1 foot 8 inches by 1 foot 8 inches. Two fragments of coping stones. The first contains an animal with a large beak like what we find on some of the capitals in the Gautamīputra cave at Nāsik. In front of it is a man in striped drawers, holding a rope which seems to have been fastened to the head of a bullock, and resting his arms on its hind-quarters.

The smaller fragment has a similar figure holding a bull by the tail. Its fore-quarters are also broken away.

No. 74.

2 feet 10 inches wide by about 4 feet high. This has been a companion slab to No. 72. It is broken away below, and the upper surfaces of all the figures split off. The carving appears to have been poor.

No. 75.

A disc 2 feet 4 inches in diameter with flanges nearly perfect. Like No. 66 it has an extra ring of creeper (*vēli*) pattern round the disc; there is a *swastika* on the upper right-hand corner.

No. 76.—See No. 39.

No. 77.

Another disc 2 feet 4 inches diameter, similar to No. 39, only that on the central raised circle or nave, instead of the usual nine or fourteen very small circles, it has the *Buddhapāda* surrounded by a ring of such circular markings. On the upper left corner has been a donative inscription, now all broken off except two letters.

Nos. 78 and 79.

See No. 39. Against the outer circle of brickwork from Nos. 73 to 82 lie a large number of broken fragments of similar discs: a lenticular bar, a piece of a coping stone, &c. On one (the lower part of a narrow pilaster ?) is a Buddha on his throne, a man to the left, and two females to the right; below are two females worshipping. The aureole behind Buddha's head rests against a large thick cushion of some sort, perhaps the foliage of the Bodhi tree.

No. 80.

2 feet 8 inches broad, by about 3 feet 6 inches high. A large flower-vase slab, has had no left side border; all the upper and right sides broken off. On the base is an inscription in a line and half, not distinct owing to the decay of the surface. It appears to read—

Damilā Kaṇhasa bhātunaṁ cha ChulakanhasaNākhāya cha(dā)na mahāche—
tiyapādamule udhaṁpato

Dr. Hultzsch renders it—"An *udhaṁpaṭo* (tablet) at the foot of the great chaitya, the gift of Kaṇha from Damila and of his brother Chulakaṇha (*i.e.*, the younger Kṛishṇa) and his sister Nākhā. (See Plate III, No. 8.)

No. 81.

2 feet 8¼ inches by 4 feet 11 inches. An upright slab, with three *triśūlas* above, having iron pins in their centres; then a fillet of creeper pattern; then three lions, the central one with an eagle's beak, all rushing to the left; then another fillet with triangular spaces. Below this to the left is a pilaster, and in the centre a dāgaba with a man and dēva on each side of it. Below is a ribbon of honeysuckle pattern.

No. 30B.

2 feet 8 inches by 5 feet 6 inches. A long slab which I dug out high up in the bank just behind No. 82. It has a pilaster down the right side, and is divided across into two large panels similarly to No. 72, of which it is a companion slab, but more perfect, as it wants only the lower right-hand corner. It has had an inscription below, rather faint now.

No. 31B.

2 feet 10 inches by about 3 feet 3 inches. A fragment of a large slab I dug out of the bank along with No. 30B. It is much injured. On the bottom is a dāgaba with two men and two *dēvas* worshipping it, as on No. 81.

No. 82.

2 feet 10 inches by 13 inches by 9 inches. This is very similar to No. 25, being part of a frieze. Below is a quadrantal moulding, then a facia with oblong holes in it; then another quadrantal member, turned up and carved with animals; then a broad dado carved at intervals with bits of highly decorated rail pattern, three uprights in each piece. In the left panel is the flaming pillar rising from the *pāda* with a figure on each side, and a worshipper kneeling below. In the panel to the right is a throne under a canopy, the *pādas* below it, and a worshipper and standing figure to the left. The uppermost member is carved with a small winding roll.

No. 83.

This is a fine double disc 2 feet 8 inches in diameter and 9 inches thick. On one side is a vine-pattern circle sloping back from the front. A few letters of inscription are indistinctly visible on the upper right corner.

No. 84.

2 feet 1 inch by 9 inches by 7 inches. A piece of frieze of a different pattern from No. 82, there being no quadrantal moulding below nor holes, and the facia carved throughout with rail pattern. The animals below it are separated from each other by a large leaf and are spiritedly cut. The uppermost member is carved with flowers in square divisions.

No. 85.

Is a thin fragment of a slab, but all the sculpture is peeled off except the seat of a throne bearing a cushion carved with a rosette. Below are the *pāda*, and on each side the feet of an attendant.

No. 32B.

A piece of a rail pillar 1 foot 3 inches broad, about 3 feet long by 4 inches thick, with only the lower disc entire.

In front of the steps down from the west gate lie a piece of a bluish slab and a lenticular bar.

No. 33B.

Forming the threshold of a door to a brick building at the west gate, is a stone 1 foot 2 inches broad and 3½ feet long, with four small circular discs on it.

No. 34B.

2 feet 4 inches broad by 2 feet 5 inches long. On the left of the entrance to the brick chapel are the *Buddhapāda* broken and plastered down with lime, showing to how late a date they were reverenced. The stone is all cracked. Round the central disc on the soles are carved figures of the *swastika*, *triśūla*, &c.

No. 35B.

Close by, on a stone 13 inches by 10 inches, are two smaller Buddhapâda 8 inches by 7½ inches, rather weatherworn.

No. 36B.

2 feet 6 inches by about 2 feet 2 inches, lying behind No. 101. A fragment of a very elaborately carved pair of the same. (See Plate XII*d*.) The *swastika*, flower vase, *triśūla* shield, and another ornament, cover the front of each foot; the compound *triśūla* and *dharma* symbol is on each toe. Round the whole at a lower level is a band carved with a creeper ornament, with a ledge outside on which has been an inscription on the front edge, nearly all illegible and part broken away—

Sidhaṁ—ha(? pa)daga ...... *pagha*

No. 37B.

In front of the brick building are many stones not numbered. One about 2 feet each way is a split portion of a coping stone containing two figures worshipping a dâgaba in the area over the roll.

No. 38B.

A fragment of a terminal coping stone with a human figure pushing the end of a roll into (or pulling it out of) the mouth of a *gaṇa*.

No. 39B.

A small piece of an upright pillar bearing the *pâda*, apparently in a boat, with a tall pillar crowned by the *dharma* symbol and two figures worshipping it on the left. There are also fragments of other figures.

Nos. 40B, 41B, and 42B.

A disc of No. 39 pattern, 2 feet 4 inches in diameter, and parts of two others.

No. 43.

About 3 feet 10 inches by 1 foot 3 inches by 6½ inches. A piece of a small rail coping stone, plain on the back, the roll carried by *gaṇa*, with rosettes in the spaces above it : much worn.

Nos, 44B$_1$ and 44B$_2$

About 2 feet by 1 foot 10 inches and 2 feet by 9½ inches. Two pieces of split coping, broken off at the left side and below. In the upper left-hand corner are two thatched houses above a long brick wall which crosses the whole field. To the right of them are two figures, apparently a man and woman, each holding a child. In front of the wall to the left is a tree with two men below it on horseback wearing the Andhra head-dress, and to the right two men with their hair cut short across their brows. Another appears below the front horse's head, and in front (to the right) below, another figure (broken) is seated. Then a very tall figure to the right, and in front of him two boys. To the right of them a woman sits on a cushion with a square fan in her left hand, and just in front of her what looks like a high wickerwork basket or seat, and on, or rather behind it, a man with his left hand on his thigh and right on his breast. Below the woman an elephant's head and *mahaut* is seen, and on the right of the stone are parts of two trees, one above the other, and a human face looking out of the bole of the lower one. The first and largest of these stones I found buried with several others in front of the west gate. The other was on the surface not many yards off and they fit on to one another. (See Plate XII*c*.)

No. 86.

Is a piece of small octagon pillar 2 feet long and 9 inches diameter, which has been cut across at no very ancient date. It bears the following inscription :—

Sidham Jaḍiṁkiyana Sidathagahapa
tisa bhariyaya Khadaya sadhutakaya
saputikaya samatukāya sabhātukāsa
sagharasutāya sakajanatihi
Bhagavāto mahachetiyapadamale
apaṇadhaṁmathāna divakhaṁbho patiṭhavito.

Dr. Hultzsch has rendered this :—

"Success! By Khadā (Skandā) the wife of the householder Sidatha of the Jadikiya (family or school) the daughter of Saghaka (?), with her daughters, with her sons, with her mother, with her brothers, (*and*) by her blood relations (?) a pillar for lamps has been erected in reverence to the great Chaitya of the holy one as a meritorious gift (*arpaṇadharma*)." (See Plate III, 9.)

No. 87.

Part split off an octagonal pillar 1 foot 6½ inches in diameter and about 4 feet 7 inches high. On each of the three sides are three panels; in the upper ones, dâgabas; in the second, standing figures of Buddha with aureoles round their heads. Below this is a broad belt, and on it, on the right-hand side, in later letters is cut—

Śrī viprajātapriyaṁ.

Near the bottom of this belt and running round all three sides in older letters is carved—

Aya Retiyā atevāsiniyā aya Dhamāya dānaṁ.

"The gift of the venerable Dhamā (Dharmā) the female disciple of the venerable Re[va]tī."[1] (See Plate IV, 10.)

Under this are three panels, one on each side, containing standing figures of Buddha with aureoles behind the heads.

No. 45B.

A thin slab with a dâgaba on it, out of which grows a pipal tree; the drum of the dâgaba has been ornamented with three figures of dâgabas. The remainder of this piece I found in the shed.

No. 46B.

About 3 feet 6 inches by 1 foot 3 inches by 6½ inches, a piece of coping stone, smaller than usual, with four lines of mediæval Nâgari writing roughly carved across it near the end.

No. 88.

This is a fine disc 2 feet 4½ inches in diameter, of the No. 39 pattern, with an extra border round it, divided into twelve sections.

No. 89.

3 feet 9 inches by 1 foot 10½ inches. A fragment of a coping stone, carved with a man holding by the tail a winged lion: its head gone.

No. 90.

2 feet 8½ inches diameter and 10 inches thick. A disc carved on both sides, the flanges chipped off.

Nos. 91, 92, 95 and 96.

These seem to be caps for pillars, 1 foot 2 inches in diameter; the fourth—1 foot 4 inches in diameter; the first has a square hole in it; the second and third round ones 3 or 4 inches deep; but the hole in the fourth is 9½ inches in diameter and goes right through the block 10 inches thick. Each is carved into a thick torus between two fillets.

No. 93.

A fragment of the base of an upright.

No. 94.

2 feet 5½ inches diameter, a disc lying close to the last, of No. 39 pattern.

---

[1] Translated by Dr. Hultzsch.

No. 97.

A rather fine body of Buddha 3 feet 3 inches high; head, arms, and toes broken off.

No. 98.

A broken disc of No. 39 pattern.

No. 99.

1 foot 3 inches by 1 foot 11 inches. A piece of a thin slab carved with a large chaitya window pattern, inside which is a poorly-carved female standing under the foliage of a tree into which she raises her right hand: weatherworn.

No. 47B.

A fragment of a *pāda*; also weatherworn.

No. 100.—See No. 39.

No. 48B.

At the west gate, just behind No. 100, I found a long narrow slab (9 feet 10 inches long) buried in a sloping position. Fully 4 feet of it is plain and has been sunk in the ground. The upper portion is carved only on one face.

Below is the throne, round-backed, with two cushions, bent legs and animal feet on them, and below it is the stool for the *pāda* (obliterated). Over it rises a pillar consisting, first, of three elephants and their riders, then a sort of water-pot moulding with five lions' heads looking out over it, then another moulding fluted on the torus, and five more heads with larger ears; then another moulding and three *gaṇa*, and above it, a fourth moulding like the second. By the throne are two worshippers on each side, one above the other; and by the elephants, two *chauri*-bearers. From each moulding spring lions, &c., with riders, and beyond each is a figure with a club. This pillar, doubtless, bore a wheel atop, but it has been broken off, as well as a piece of the right side.

No. 49B.

Beside the last was also dug up a small piece of thin plain coping-stone with a fragment of a two-line inscription on it.

No. 101.

An octagonal finial 1 foot 3¼ inches diameter, with a chaitya window on the four principal sides and a female bust in each.

No. 102.

About 1 foot 5 inches each way. Apparently a *Śālika* or worshipping figure; but the head, &c., is broken off. (See Plate XII*a*.)

No. 103.

The remains of a much-injured double disc.

No. 104.

2 feet 10 inches by 4 feet 7 inches high. A flower-vase slab in pretty perfect condition.

The numbers painted on 86, 90, 97, 102, 104, 107, 115, 117, 205, &c., are so placed as to injure their appearance.

No. 50B.

A slab 2 feet 9 inches broad with three *dharma* symbols above having iron pins in their centres; under them a band with floral devices, and below it three tigers.....

No. 105.

1 foot 9 inches by 1 foot 6 inches. A fragment having, on the back, part of a fat *gaṇa*, and part of a disc of two broad rings of leaves round the central core.

No. 106.

1 foot 6½ inches by 1 foot 11 inches. A very similar piece, but almost entire; seems to have been an old small rail bar with a rosette on one side. Afterwards a dancing *gaṇa* has been carved lengthwise on the curved back.

No. 51B.

1 foot 4 inches by 2 feet. Somewhat like No. 99, but much better carving. The female in the area holds a heavy jewel in her right hand, which she is about to attach to the left ear. Her drapery is not abundant but is artistically represented. (See Plate XII*b*.)

No. 107.

2 feet 9½ inches by 4 feet 5 inches. Another slab with flower-vase, similar to No. 104 : not broken.

No. 108.

Is another plain cross-bar on the side of which a *gaṇa* has been carved. It is smaller than No. 106 and only carved on the back.

Nos. 109, 110, and 111.

Three discs carved on one side, with three tiers of petals round the central area, like No. 39.

No. 112.

1 foot 4½ inches diameter. A fine disc with outer creeper border. At the lower left corner has been an inscription weathered off except—

. . . . . *nasa*
. . . . *latasa*
. . . . . *isa*

A small dāgaba has been roughly drawn in the centre of it.

No. 113.

This is the only monolithic lion left seated on his hind legs; his forelegs are broken off.

No. 52B.

A single foot (rather part of one) may belong to it (No. 113).

No. 53B.

Two forefeet, also beside it (No. 113), certainly belong to another animal.

No. 114.

2 feet 4½ inches diameter. A large fragment of a single disc with an inscription (See Plate IV, 13) on the upper right-hand corner nearly complete—

Budhala gahapatiputasa Haranikasa-
sidhaṭhasa samitanānibadhavasā suyi
dānaṁ.

No. 115.

2 feet 8 inches by 4 feet 3 inches by 7 inches. An upright slab, same style as No. 81.

No. 116.

A broken disc. See No. 39.

No. 117.

2 feet 11 inches by 4 feet 5 inches. A flower-vase slab, lower left corner broken off. Compare Nos. 1 and 107. It does not appear to have had an inscription. This leans against a brick dāgaba.

No. 118.

About 4 feet 3 inches by 2 feet 5 inches. A fragment of a split coping stone. In the area over the roll to the right is a dāgaba with a double *chhatra* and two worshippers. In the next above, only one of the worshippers is left. Under the roll is a man bearing it.

No. 54B.

1 foot 7 inches by 10½ inches and about 4 feet high. The lower portion of an inner rail pillar, with lower half disc and parts of three fillets above it. This is to the right of the brick dāgaba.

No. 119.

A small fragment of a coping stone, showing the male bearer below the roll and a man worshipping a tree above on the left.

No. 55B.

2 feet 5 inches diameter. A fine single disc, very entire. There has been a short inscription on the upper corner of the right-hand tenon, but it is abraded except a letter or two.

No. 120.

About 1 foot 10 inches each way. The upper right-hand corner of a slab with the *Dharmachakra* on it, and a *dēva* and two human figures to the right of it.

No. 56B.

A fragment, about 4 feet long, of a split coping stone: has been carved with an elephant, man, and tiger, sharply cut.

No. 121.

3 feet 7 inches by 1 foot 11 inches by 8½ inches, and another about 2 feet by 3 feet. Two broken stones, exactly similar, forming parts of a slab with two offsets on each edge and at one end, as if for some coping. There has been a large circular hole through the slab, by which it has been broken. On one edge is part of an inscription in two lines, one of the most interesting yet found. (See Plate IV, 11.)

Pandit Bhagvānlāl Indraji has supplied me with the following transcript and Sanskrit and English translations :—[1]

[1] [*Si*]*dhaṁ Raño Vāsiṭhiputasa Sāmi Siri Pulumāvisa savachharaṁ* . . . . . . *piṁdasutariyānaṁ Kahutaragahapatisa Purigahapatisa cha putasa Isilasa sabhātukasa*..

[1] Dr. Hultzsch's translation is substantially the same as the Pandit's, but was only received after this was in type.

[2] *sa(bha ?)ginikasa bhayāya chasa Nākanikāya saputakasa* . . . . . [? *Bhagava*]*to mahāchetiye chetakiyā-nam nikā*[*ya*]*sa parigahe aparadāre dhamachaka dedhammam* [*mātā*] *pitu* [*udisa* ?]

In Sanskrit.

[1] *Siddham Rājno Vāsishṭhīputrasya Svāmi Śrī-Pulumavek samvatsara* . . . . *piṇḍasūtrīyayoh Kahutaragrahapateh Purīgrahapateśchaputrasya Ṛishilasya sabhrātṛikasya.*
[2] *sa(bha)ginikasya bhāryāyāśchāsya Nāginikāyāḥ saputrakasya* . . . . . *Bhagavato mahāchaitye chaityakā-nam nikāyasya parigrahe aparadvare dharmachakram deyadharmah matāpitarāvuddiśya.*

Translation.

"Hail![1] In the year . . . . . of the illustrious lord the king Pulumâvi, son of the Vāsishṭha (mother). The merit of the gift of a *Dhammachaka* (Wheel of the Law) on the western-doorway in the great Chaitya of Bhagavat (Buddha) in possession of the Chetika school by two Piṇḍasūtris—the householder Kahutara and Isila, the son of the householder Puri, with his brother, his sister, his wife Nāganikā with (*their*) son."

The first of the two fragments of this inscription I discovered at the western gateway, and deciphering the portions of the letters left in the first line, made search for the rest, which I found about 20 yards to the north, among many chips. It was numbered '121.' The small fragment still wanting was sought for in vain. These stones are well worth preservation.

The value of this inscription I recognized as soon as I discovered it: it proves beyond a doubt that the Amarāvati Stūpa was either already built, or was being built during the reign of the great Pulumâvi, whose inscriptions we have at Nāsik, at Kārle, and on the Sanchi gateway, and this indicates that this stupa was already in existence in the second century A.D. if not earlier.

The statement that it belonged to the Chetika school (if supported) is also of some interest. The Buddhists early divided into two great schools, the Mahāsāṁghika or 'great congregation,' composed of old and young alike, known in China as 'the school of various and miscellaneous moral rules;' and the school of the Sthaviras or 'of the old men,' which acknowledges the authority of the original *Vinaya* only. From the Mahāsāṁghikas sprung numerous schools, among which was that of the Chetikas[2] (Sanskrit *Chaitika*). So far as the sculptures left at Amarāvati testify, they do not seem to have gone the length of the later Mahāyāna sects in the adoration of images of Buddha, and no trace has yet been found of the worship of Avalōkitēśvara or the Bōdhisattwas; the dāgaba, the Bodi tree, the Buddhapāda, and the Dharmachakra are the prevalent objects of reverence here. Scenes from the life of Buddha are represented, but in such minor positions that they do not warrant us in supposing they were intended for worship. One broken statue of Buddha, however, has been found, and may have been worshipped. Though the Nāga figures prominently on the dāgaba slabs, no fragment of one has been found elsewhere.

No. 122 (Sewell's No. 25).

9 feet 9 inches by 2 feet 2 inches by 1 foot. A coping stone, plain on one side, with the roll pattern supported by dwarfs: much abraded on the other side.

No. 123 (Sewell's No. 26).

2 feet 3 inches broad by about 2 feet 6 inches above ground. The base of a pillar, apparently *in situ*. The lower half disc only entire, the back quite plain.

No. 124 (Sewell's No. 27).

A disc. See No. 39.

No. 125 (Sewell's No. 28).

Another base of a pillar, apparently *in situ*; front half disc, broken at the edges, back plain.

---

[1] The Pandit translates *Siddham* 'To the perfect one,' but see *Ind. Ant.* Vol. X, p. 273.
[2] Perhaps the same at the Chaitiyavādā or Chaityaśaila school. See Vassilief, and *Ind. Ant.* Vol. IX, pp. 300, 301.

No. 126 (Sewell's No. 34).

About 2 feet 9 inches by 4 feet 6 inches.[1] The base of a pillar of the outer rail in which large hollows have been made for grinding in. Below the half disc is a border of flower pattern, in the middle compartment over it has been a dāgaba and worshippers, and in each side compartment human figures. On the back is a half disc and flower border below it.

No. 127 (Sewell's No. 35 ?).

6 feet 3 inches by 2 feet 2 inches by 1 foot. A coping stone, nearly entire; plain on the back. The roll is upheld by three fat *gaṇa*, and half discs fill the area as above; below them on the roll are small square plaques with two birds and flowers in each.

No. 128.

4 feet 9 inches by 2 feet 2 inches by 1 foot 1½ inches. A coping stone of the same pattern as the last. It has been a terminal one, and has a fat *gaṇa* at the left end, with a heavy bead hung on a string about his neck: he is drawing a sort of rope out of his mouth, which goes into the left end of the roll. Another similar figure, also with striped drawers, sits under the first upward coil. On the bend below the half disc is a cobra's head between two birds.

No. 129 (Sewell's No. 38 ?).

About 3 feet each way. The lower portion of a flower-vase slab. The base, with most of the inscription, has been broken off.

No. 130.

This is the upper portion of No. 129.

No. 131.

This has been a slab similar to No. 115, &c.; the lower part is broken off, leaving the top of the dāgaba.

No. 132 (Sewell's No. 33 ?).

About 3 feet by 2 feet 5 inches. Part of a split coping stone. The roll comes out of the mouth of a *makara* at the lower right-hand corner. Above it is a tree over a throne and a man presenting some large object. A man supports the roll, and on the next space above it is a throne with *pāda* under it and a *chauri*-bearer, but the *dharmachakra* is broken away. On the roll below is a medallion carved with an ornamented dāgaba.

No. 133 (Sewell's No. 45).

5 feet 2 inches by 1 foot 11 inches by 10 inches. A coping stone, plain on the back, and on the front a bull pursuing a man who catches a winged deer by the hind leg. Above is a belt of elaborate floral pattern.

No. 134 (Sewell's No. 36).

1 foot 2¼ inches by 1 foot 11 inches by 6½ inches. Another piece of the same pattern: represents a man seizing a winged tiger by the ear, and with a sort of sickle in his other hand.

No. 135 (Sewell's No. 37).

Is the smashed base of a pillar with plain back, perhaps *in situ*.

---

[1] Sewell says 6 feet.

No. 136 (Sewell's No. 44).

A disc of No. 39 pattern.

No. 137 (Sewell's No. 39).

Another smashed base of a pillar.

No. 138 (Sewell's No. 40).

2 feet 6 inches by 4 feet 10 inches by 6½ inches. The lower portion of a pillar consisting of the lower half disc and border and three plain flutes above, also the edge of the middle disc. Mr. Sewell says 6 feet 1 inch long.

No. 139 (Sewell's No. 42).

2 feet 7 inches by 3 feet 4 inches by 11 inches. The upper portion of a very richly carved pillar, with a fragment of a tenon on the top. The uppermost belt of carving has a dwarf at each end, from whose mouths a creeper proceeds and is carried across with four pairs of animals between. Below this is the upper half disc, the outer border of which is very richly carved with flowers and birds : inside it is a simple leaf pattern, and in the central area is a tree beyond a platform on which are two *pāda* : on each side sit three men, and underneath them are two others on each side in horizontal positions.

Below the half disc and between it and the upper edge of the central disc are three panels. In the central one is a large arch-roofed canopy with a rail pattern base, and open at the sides, carried by shafts on the shoulders of four *gana*. Inside is an elephant ; and at each end are two figures, one with an umbrella carried over him. In the side compartments is a flying figure in the upper corner of each ; below are three standing figures, one on the left side with a flag, one in the right with a torch ; below, on each side are two figures dancing or running, and at the same time saluting the elephant. (See Plate XIII.)

The back of the stone has a half disc, and over it a tree with the *pādas* at the foot of it and two elephants, approaching it from each side. Below the disc the stone is split off.

No. 140 (Sewell's No. 41).

2 feet 2 inches by about 5 feet 1 inch. This has been a corner upright, the left margin of the stone being slightly recessed to receive the edge of a similar stone ; but a portion seems to have been split off the right edge ; for the lower half disc is incomplete, and only two of the usual three panels are left above, each containing a dwarf, much damaged.

On the back, the central compartment is nearly entire. On the left side of it is a tree, and at its root a large white-ants' nest. A figure behind points down to it ; another on his knees in front seems to have hold of a snake, while another snake is wriggling towards him. Behind, to the right, are three men and a child. The compartments right and left have contained human figures, but are much damaged. Below is a half disc with a florid border and carved differently from the usual pattern. Below this is a broad vine-pattern border.

No. 141 (Sewell's No. 43).

This is a large piece of rail broken into three pieces. It has been much abraded, and had the roll with half discs on one side and was smooth on the back. It also had an inscription, of which only a very few letters can now be read.

No. 142.

This is a middle fragment of a rail pillar containing the greater part of a disc which has a border of six-petalled flowers or stars round it. The base of this pillar stands close beside it. It was unbroken at the close of the excavations, when photographs were taken.

No. 143 (Sewell's No. 46).

8 feet 8 inches by 2 feet 7 inches by 1 foot 1 inch. This is a large coping stone. Over the first bend of the roll on the right is a dāgaba with a multitude of flower-shaped umbrellas over it ; a rāja

on the centre of the drum, a *chakra* on the right, and a tree on the left. Under the roll is a double rope, and while a man in each division bears up the former, a woman carries the latter.

In the second bight is a sort of high pedestal, on the top of which are three dwarfs. On a square boss upon the roll below are three or four human figures.

In the third bight is a winged *Garuḍa*, his tail over his head, a five-hooded snake held by the neck in his mouth, and its body seized by his talons. Below on a round boss is a star formed of three *triśūlas*.

In the fourth bight is a pedestal held up by three dwarfs with three fox-headed figures springing out of it. Below is a square boss with florid ornamentation. At the left end is a tree and a figure worshipping it: perhaps another is broken off below with a piece of the slab. Above and below the larger carving is a belt of creepers.

There is a large mortise hole about 2 feet from the right end, and a smaller one near the left.

The other side is also carved, and, though somewhat weatherworn, all the details can easily be made out, and form a most interesting series.

On the left is an in-door scene in a two-storeyed house or palace. Below, in the left corner, a man with a high head-dress sits with two attendants behind him; another sits on a cushion in front talking to him, and behind are two others with high head-dresses, each with his left hand across his chest. Beyond a pillar to the right, in an end room or doorway, are two men standing in earnest conversation. In the upper storey to the left are two women in separate rooms, the one with her hands clasped, the second resting her head on her right hand as if in grief. In the end compartment are two more, apparently conversing.

The next scene has a lady seated on the left with *chauri* and *chhatra* bearers behind her, and what looks like the large oval disc or fan seen over the heads of rājas in other sculptures. In front of her, to the right, stand two females, and behind them a third. A fourth enters from a door on the upper right side of the scene, apparently carrying a dish. In front of her below is one playing on a flute, with two others perhaps dancing in front of the Rāṇī. In the near foreground are four women seated and playing on musical instruments.

In the centre of the third and largest scene is an empty throne with a cushioned back over which two priestly heads project, and behind them is the sacred tree with the triple umbrella over it. Beneath the throne is a stool on a cushion, bearing the *pāda*. A female on the left of it bends in profound adoration; behind her another pushes forward a little boy to worship it. Behind this second, a third advances with her hand on a dwarf's head and a fourth follows her. Close to the throne on the left is also a *chauri*-bearer, a female. Above are two male and two female *dēvatās* flying towards the tree. To the right of the *pāda* are three men seated, and behind them two tall men come in through a *stūpa* or *toraṇa* gate, outside which is a man holding the bridle of a horse with a rider on it, and beyond are two young heads. To the right of them again are buildings. Above, to the right of the tree, are three flying figures—one at least a female. A dwarf or *Gandharva* is over the *toraṇa* gate and two more are in the air to the right.

The last scene to the right is also an interior one. In the upper portion are five seated figures, apparently worshipping an empty throne. Below the three, to the right, are two tiers of roofs, each bearing a worn inscription (see Plate IV, No. 14). Under this is a female on a bed with an infant, and a woman attending on each side the bed.

No. 144.

1 foot 7 inches by 10 inches by about 4 inches. On the inner side of the path the upright base of a pillar, the smooth side facing outwards, and with the remains of plaster on the inner side, but so following the surface of the flutes as to show that it was probably painted over. Fragments of it also remain in the circles of the plain half disc at the foot.

No. 57B.

A fine double disc lying inside the circle, which, however, has lost its tenons and is chipped a good deal round the margins.

No. 145 (Sewell's No. 78).

About 3 feet 6 inches by 2 feet 9 inches by 1 foot. A corner slab of the coping; has a large flat dwarf in the middle, into whose mouth a man is forcing the end of the roll; his head is decorated with flowers and a man is seen behind pulling his ear, another behind the roll helping the one in front. Over the roll to the right are three elephants supporting a large base or *howdah*, on which is a flower vase or some such object.

The other side of this slab has an inscription on the round—

-k(a)ligāya mahachetiye utarāyāke unisa dānaṁ.

"Gift of a coping stone at the north-gate of the great Chaitya of Kalinga (?) .."

but the greater part of the *k* and several letters before it have been broken off since Mr. Sewell first unearthed it. (See Plate IV, 15.)

A high brick-built tower or other erection, with three arched windows on as many faces, divides the area into two panels. On the right is an interior: a rāja with three nearly nude attendants behind his throne, one with a *chauri*, and another with a large oval object having a line down its longer diameter. Below, on each side, is a female seated on a stool, and below them other two on the floor.

In the upper portion of the left panel a large elephant is entering, and a man is apparently cutting off one of his tusks. Behind is a figure whose face is gone; to the right is a small figure and three men below. Perhaps this represented the Chhadanta Jātaka.

The carving of this slab is of unusual excellence.

No. 146 (Sewell's No. 79).

About 2 feet by 3 feet, is the upper portion of a pillar of the outer rail: it has part of a tenon on the top. The upper belt of ornamentation (see Plate XV*a*) has had four pairs of animals, tigers, cows, two mythic animals, and two broken away, all carved with unusual spirit. The upper half disc has a creeper border round it. Part of the portion below is also entire and sculptured, but sunk in the ground.

On the back was a dāgaba, partly destroyed, and a winged lion approaching it. About half of the half disc is left on this side.

No. 147 (Sewell's No. 80).

3 feet 6 inches by 1 foot 9 inches by 1 foot 2 inches. A fragment of a coping stone very much damaged. It has been carved on both sides; on the back only the *makāra* is left with the end of the roll in his mouth.

In front is a woman kneeling in reverence to a figure seated cross-legged in front of a round thatched hut. Beyond her are two males, also reverencing him, and beyond them either a domed hut or a dāgaba of very plain type. There have been also some other figures now destroyed.

No. 148 (Sewell's No. 82).

3 feet 10 inches by 2 feet 7 inches by 1 foot 2 inches. Another piece of coping. The roll ornament is upheld by human figures. In the area above it is a dāgaba with two worshippers, and below, on a medallion, is the sacred wheel over the throne, with two attendants.

On the other side, to the left, is Buddha on a throne under a tree, and a tall *chauri*-bearer to the right, swinging the *chauri* with vigour. Behind him are five male figures worshipping under a tree, the two in front seated. A thin division is marked in the conventional way in which the Buddhists indicate rocks, and beyond it are four priests and some other figures worshipping a Buddha, of whom only a fragment is left.

No. 149 (Sewell's No. 83).

This is a double disc 2 feet 9½ inches in diameter, somewhat weatherworn.

No. 150 (Sewell's No. 84).

2 feet 10 inches wide by 2 feet 2 inches high. The middle section of a pillar of the outer rail, with a disc on the back and the greater part of a most elaborately carved circle in front. At the bottom is the throne and cushions, below it the *pāda*, on each side a deer; from behind it rises a massive pillar ornamented with two sets of three each of flying-fox heads and busts, such as we find on friezes, &c. Above is the abacus that has supported the sacred wheel now broken away. On each side behind the

throne is a *chauri*-bearer with high turban, and the whole remaining field is filled with rājas doing reverence. Twenty-one figures are still left or traceable, and the feet of a female to the left of the abacus.

No. 151 (Sewell's No. 20).

10 feet 8 inches by 2 feet 7 inches by 11½ inches. A large coping stone lying on the back outside the circle. Five men support the flower roll on the outside. On the first area on the left is a dāgaba with two worshippers, and below it a medallion with the tree over the throne and a woman on each side of it. In the second area is the wheel on the pillar behind the throne and two *chauri*-bearers in attendance; below is a square plaque worn nearly smooth. In the third is a dāgaba and attendants, and on the medallion below is what appears to be a vase on a stand with four worshippers. In the fourth are three stout fat worshipping figures rising from a short octagon stand crowned with leaves.

The inner side of this magnificent slab has been miserably destroyed by village boys pelting it with stones.

On the left are several people coming out of a large group of buildings to the right. Above, to the right of these, is a lofty state palanquin carried by fat dwarf figures. Still to the right are two men riding on non-descript animals, and a third below them; also two men about to enter a building to the right in which is the throne over the *pāda*, and behind it two attendants and the stem of a tree, the foliage of which comes through the roof and is spread over the round of the stone. To the right of it is the fiery pillar over the throne; three figures flying on *śārdūlas*, &c., and numerous men and dwarfs below. The last compartment to the right has a king seated on a throne with numerous attendants around him (all injured). On the upper part of the stone is an inscription in a long line, which appears to read—

—patino ida saduhutuya gharaniya Kanhaya duhutuya apāsikāya kamāya saputikaya sabhatukāya sabhaginikāya bhikhuniya bhanāgamata . . . . ya . . . . . .

No. 152.

Part of a disc 2 feet 9 inches diameter, with a very pretty outer border and a small dāgaba with *chhatris* carved in the centre: the back has been split off.

No. 153.

Very similar to the last, but more weatherworn.

No. 154.

2 feet 9 inches by 1 foot 4 inches by 1 foot. A fragment of rail coping. On the outer side is left only three dwarfs that were probably on the *makara's* head. On the inner side are two small compartments. That at the right end contains a woman carrying a man huck-a-back, and another female behind her. In the next a woman is bent down at a man's feet, who holds her by the hand and lays his other hand on her back; behind are two women, one with her hands joined. To the left, in another compartment, is a flying figure whose head is broken away.

No. 155.

2 feet 8 inches by about 6 feet 6 inches. A pillar of the outer rail, broken at the top, smooth on the back, but with the greater portion of the central and lower discs left. Under the latter is a band of pretty geometrical pattern. (Plate XV*c*.)

No. 156.

Another rail pillar, higher than the last, smooth on the back and the front entirely destroyed, except the band below the lower half disc. (Plate XV*b*.)

No. 157.

2 feet 10 inches by 5 feet by 10 inches. The lower portion of a fine upright of the outer rail, broken into three pieces. The one piece about 5 feet high, the other half being broken across the middle. The band below the half disc on the back is unusually broad and richly carved. The outer

band of the disc is divided into small ovals containing leaves, flowers, birds, and tigers. Above the disc are three dwarfs.

On the front is an equally fine half disc, and above it, in the middle, the *pāda* at the foot of the flaming pillar with two worshippers. On the right are three male figures, and on the left another flaming pillar with worshippers.

No. 58B.

Is the base of another pillar of the rail; the lower half disc is only partially complete. The back is smooth except a fragment of an inscription—

Kojasa chakapato [*dāna*].
"A tablet bearing a wheel [the gift] of Koja (Kubja?)"—(Dr. Hultzsch).

No. 158.

About 4 feet by 2 feet 4 inches. A fragment of the head of a rail pillar with a broad band of animals over the half disc. Below it is a gateway near the middle of the area and two ladies entering from it to the right to a rāja seated with an oval disc behind his head, a female fanning him, and another behind him, while two others are seated at his feet.

To the left of the gate a man is being carried in the arms of another, while other three accompany them, all woolly haired. In the background a fat figure is clasped round the neck by another behind until he seems about to choke; and to the left a female is being carried away on the back of another to a building which is mostly broken off.

No. 159.

2 feet 8 inches by about 5 feet. The lower half of a rail pillar with a fragment of neat fret pattern round the central disc.

No. 160.

This is a small fragment of a split coping stone. Over the flower roll has been the throne and sacred wheel with two attendants.

No. 161.

About 4 feet 3 inches by 2 feet 7 inches by 1 foot. A larger piece of coping. In the left compartment is a female on a couch with very heavy anklets; behind is a half-open door and a man stands beyond; another at the foot seems speaking: below and in front of him stands another with perhaps two spears; he appears also to address either the lady or a man who stands in front of the head of the couch. Below it are two women crouching over a large seat; and in front of it a third sits with her left hand to her cheek, with her hair half loose, while a fourth with a round *tilaka* on her brow lies along below.

On the back is the usual roll upborne by human figures; and in one space is a dāgaba with male and female worshippers, placed in a sort of boat and surrounded at the base by small harpy-like figures with the fox heads found on several stones here.

No. 162.

Is a double disc 2 feet 6½ inches in diameter, somewhat damaged on the back.

No. 163.

About 2 feet by 2 feet 10 inches. The lower left-hand portion of a flower-vase slab. It has had an inscription in three lines at the bottom, but very few syllables of it can be made out.

No. 164.

About 5 feet by 2 feet 10 inches. The lower half of a rail pillar at a corner; the mortises for the cross-bars being at the side of one face and on the edge. On the first side is a pedestal with the *pāda* below it and a male attendant on each side; above the pedestal are some letters scratched in not very old Pāli characters, but indistinct.

On the other and broader side, a well-cut band of flower pattern extends between two *makaras* below the half disc, which has also a very neat leaf-pattern margin. (See Plate XV, 2.) In the central flute above, a very fat male is seated addressing a figure on the floor before him with a rather peculiar mop-like head of hair, on whose head another with loose and thick hair leans. Other figures have filled up the panel, of which the top is broken off.

In the left compartment is a male with crimped hair kneeling before a tall female: behind him is a stout figure, whose head and shoulders are broken off.

On the right side panel is the same kneeling figure and parts of three men. one with a bow in his hand.

No. 165.

This is a double disc of the rail, 2 feet 7 inches diameter, somewhat chipped. (Plate XV*d*.)

No. 166.

A fragment of the base of a pillar which has had a very pretty band below the half disc.

No. 167.

Is a portion of a pillar of the outer rail standing about 7 feet above the ground, but the upper portion and one side have been hammered to atoms, apparently quite lately. The north side was intended for the inner side, so that it cannot now be *in situ*.

A fine creeper band crossed the stone under the lower half circle, which had five circles of petals and a neat border. Over this the left panel has been knocked off; a part of a figure in curious checked dress only is left. In the middle panel three figures out of four are left, wanting the heads; they wear long, loose, checked dresses reaching from the neck to the ankles, unlike any found elsewhere, and seem to advance to the right towards hills and a tree. The hills and tree reappear in the left of the right panel, where are two men, each with his arm round the other, and one touching a face which comes out of what is, perhaps, a dāgaba with a tree on the top of it. Over their heads is a man flying in the same checked dress as in the preceding compartments.

Over this was a richly-carved panel, but more than half of it has been smashed to pieces. In the middle was a throne, apparently with a tree rising up behind it, and 15 figures are still recognizable as males worshipping it, three of them *dēvatas*. Scarcely two head-dresses are alike and the countenances all differ. It is a great pity that this slab has been so destroyed.

The other side is very much abraded, but had only the usual three *gaṇa* between the discs.

No. 168.

This is half of a disc, weatherworn, and the back split off.

No. 169.

A pillar in the north gate 13¼ inches by 10½ inches, and about 3 feet above the surface. On the north or outer-side is carved part of a flower vase, recently damaged on the top.

No. 170.

14½ inches by 9¾ inches, and standing about 2 feet above the ground. The lower portion of another pillar with a face and arms on the outer side: also much damaged.

No. 59B.

A base 1 foot 9¼ inches by 1 foot 11 inches, with two thin plinths below and the bowl-shaped member above (much broken), into which was let a pillar about a foot square, the base being open on the side next the wall to allow the pillar to touch it. It now stands on a flag of blue limestone forming a third plinth below it, and at about the same level as the flag stones of the great circle.

No. 171.

2 feet 9 inches by about 7 feet above ground, of which 18 inches below is rough. A slab of the outer rail, like No. 167, a good deal broken in excavating. It has, as usual, a band of scroll and leaf ornament between two *makaras* at the bottom under the lower half disc. (See Plate XV*f*.) Above this are three panels: in the central one a rāja is seated under a tree on the right, with some object in his lap, and a female on either side. He is reverencing either a bird—a peacock—in front of him, or a figure seated in the air just above it.

The left panel is too much destroyed to make out its contents. A tree appears in the right of it also, and a female kneels to some one on a seat.

On the right a rāja has apparently gone to sleep on his throne; behind it are two females with chauri and long oval disc, probably a fan; he has tied his cloth round his kness to give him support. Below, on a large round seat with footstool, is a man with a sword across his knees and some one supplicating him.

The large circular disc above has been full of figures, now nearly all destroyod. On a large throne in the centre, with a footstool in front of it, sat a rāja and two queens; another sits on a large round seat to the right, one foot on a soft cushion on the floor. She wears two heavy rings on each ankle, but has also a sock, figured in lozenge pattern, which reaches up to the middle of the leg. To the left sits a female with her hair in a long-knotted coil hanging down her back and some object between her hands, perhaps bread. The lower portion of the circle is filled with water-plants and birds; all above is destroyed.

The back of the stone has the usual flower band under the half disc. Above it are two *gaṇas* in the central compartment, and one in each side; and the disc in the middle has been of quite a different pattern from the usual ones. A large area in the centre has been filled with three harpy figures (nearly unrecognizable now); the petal rings are narrow and only two of them. Outside them is a sort of honeysuckle border, and outside that, one formed of four ornamental ropes or rolls, joined at eight points by clasps or medallions.

No. 172.

This is a small fragment of the base of what must have been a richly-carved pillar; the back is split off.

No. 173.

A fragment of a double disc.

No. 174.

A disc 3 feet 8 inches diameter. The back is much damaged; so also is the front, but so much is left as to make it still a very interesting slab when the relation of the different figures can be traced out. At the top is a building, apparently intended to represent three sides of a square with arched ends. On the roof of this is an inscription in three lines which reads—

Gahapatisa Budhinoputasa Makābudhino sapi-
tukasa sabhaginikasa sabhāriyasa
deyadhaṁa parichikā be suchiya dānā:

This "gift of two rails, by Makabudhi to son of Budhi and his father, sisters and wife" however, throws no light on the subject of the sculpture. On the lower part of the scene towards the left a lady is seated on a semicircular-backed chair, surrounded by quite a group of others, and one is entering from a doorway behind her carrying some dish. On the extreme right is a man on horseback entering from another gateway; with him is one carrying two spears, and in front of him several others, some with blouses, and one of them carrying an umbrella over the head of a tall figure just in front of the horse. There are about twenty-five figures in this disc.

No. 175.

This is a small fragment of a coping stone bearing the remains of a portion of an inscription (see Plate IV, 16) which reads—

(Si)dhaṁ Sulasagahapatiputena gahapa[*ti*]. . .
-nāgatāya bālikena ya Sulasena sadhūtu . . . .
[*da*]*khinapasedāra kārita deyadhama.*

Dr. Hultzsch translates this:—

"Success! A gate, a meritorious gift, was caused to be made on the southern side ... by the householder ..., the son of the householder Sulasa, and by Sulasa (*his*) son of ... *nāgatā*, together with his daughters."

No. 176.

Is the base of a corner rail pillar, but is so damaged, perhaps in excavating, that little is left except the band below the half circle at the base on the inner side.

No. 60B.

This is a piece of what has been a very fine dāgaba slab, but it has been broken to pieces long ago.

No. 177.

2 feet 3 inches by about 4 feet. Part of a semicircular slab with four steps round it, each about 2⅜ inches broad and 2 inches high; it has had a semicircular hole in the centre; and as the upper surface is rough to within 2 inches of the edge, it must have supported some image.

No. 178 (Two pieces).

About 4½ feet by 1 foot 9 inches by 1 foot, and a smaller portion joining on below. Pieces of coping stone much worn. On the right has been a flaming pillar, with rocks to the left of it and a horse and elephant approaching. Below is a long building and two heads in front of it. To the left is a throne, and over it a *torana* gateway, with the *triśūla* apparently in flames, just over the back of the throne. Above, to the left, two men on an elephant approach the gate; below, in a house, are three men; still lower to the left are four. Above them is a high brick wall with several angles, and beyond this is too much broken to be made out.

No. 61B.

This large slab I turned up to the east of No. 178. The style of art is different from that of the general run of the slabs, being much ruder. It is carved with only two figures. To the right is a man with a high turban, a very heavy earring in the right, and a square one in the left ear, with a heavy necklace having two square clasps on it and heavy bracelets. His *langoti* is tied round the waist by a scarf with rich ends. His toes are turned right and left, and he holds up a flower with his left hand, while the right rests on the head of a boy behind him. This boy has also heavy earrings, a collar and *langoti*, and he holds a flower in his left hand. Both have oblique eyes. They stand on what appears to be a brick wall.

No. 179 (Sewell's No. 13).

7 feet 3 inches by 2 feet 7 inches. A slab of the coping lying in the inner circle. At the left end the sculpture is entirely peeled off. What is left at the right presents part of a very animated battle scene, with chariots, horses, elephants, &c. From a chariot, open behind, the warrior is throwing his javelin at the pursuing foe. An elephant has seized a horse by the neck and holds him fast, while his rider may attack the horseman at pleasure; another horse goes down upon his head and the rider is trying to save himself from being thrown forward, while beyond him is a horseman at full speed. In another chariot are two men, one with a bow.

It is a great pity this remarkable scene is so injured; all the finer details, even of what is left, are worn away or split off.

No. 179 *B* and *C*.

The first of these is the base of a nearly square pillar, and the second the bottom of a rail pillar, perhaps *in situ*. There is no carving on either: both have suffered in the excavation. There is a similar base of a rail pillar behind a piece of brick wall or basement, a little further round, about half way to No. 180.

No. 180.

Is the base of a rail pillar *in situ*, of which the sculpture has been all but entirely cleared off, apparently quite recently. A little bit of the pattern of the lower band is left on the back only.

No. 181.

Another pillar base *in situ*, which has also suffered severely, but a part of the lower disc is left on the front.

No. 182.

This is a double disc, with a fragment of an inscription on the upper left corner. In the centre of the circle is a throne with the *pāda* below and the tree behind: two tall *chauri*-bearers are behind the throne, and the whole area is filled by about 29 other figures. The back is elaborately carved in the usual style.

No. 183.

This is a disc from which the front has peeled off. There is a fragment of an inscription on the upper left corner—

. . . . . . kayasamanikāya
-saghamitāya sabhā :.
[duhu]tukāya sabha-
[g]inikāya
-danaṁ

The peeled surface has some rude drawing on it and some comparatively modern inscriptions in *Devanagari*.

No. 184.

This with Nos. 185, 186, 191,194 are *in situ*, but have been mercilessly treated. Only a portion of the lower disc of this rail pillar is left.

No. 185.

This is a double disc with parts of an inscription on the upper left corner—

-chi kayasa manikiya
-(ya ?) sabhaginikāya
. . . na.

No. 186.

Base of a rail pillar. The whole of the half disc on the back and most of that on the front is left. The small fragments of the disc between this and the next pillar lie where it has been broken up.

No. 187.

This is a fragment of the lower half of a rail pillar split up the middle and out of its position. The front is split off.

No. 188.

9 feet 3½ inches by 2 feet 8 inches by 1 foot 1 inch. This is a large coping stone, slightly curved, with the flower roll supported by human figures on the outer side. The inner side is a good deal weather-worn, but contains at least five scenes. Beginning from the left hand we have in the first a building, at the entrance to which a figure is seated with his back to the spectator; to the right is a *Nāgarāja* and three other men in front, also a small female figure supporting some large oblong object on her shoulder. Behind these are seen six heads, of which three at least have the simple Nāga hood, indicative of females, and it has been probably over two of the others also, but is decayed. From a balcony at the very top of the scene three figures look down.

To the right is an irregular division, and the next scene begins with a female standing among rocks or on steps, holding up the palm of her left hand as if speaking of the scene below, and just in front of her, to the left, are two heads looking down over the hind quarters of a horse towards the Nāgarāja, who, with his hands joined, appears in the lower part of the scene advancing to the right; behind is a horse bearing two riders, both of whose toes are turned backwards, and the face and body of the hindmost rider. The horse is leaping over a little fat figure, lying, perhaps asleep. Behind it is another figure looking down and holding a spear or other similar weapon. In front of the horse is a rocky wall or division reaching half-way up the scene, to where the division is carried horizontally to the right, making room for four figures over it, two of them with weapons, who seem rushing to the right, but are looking back at the riders or at the little figure below. Over all the figures from the *Nāgarāja* are three men mounted, the first on a horse, the second on an animal with an aquiline beak and feline claws, and the third on one with a tiger's head. Between each pair is a figure with a sword, broadest near the point, similar to those which figure so often in the Ajanta paintings.

Below the horizontal division line just mentioned, under a tree, are two figures seated, one apparently receiving something from the other. Just behind the second of these a tall man has seized another by the middle and is pitching him head foremost into the turmoil on the right.

In the lower portion of the next compartment a man riding on a deer is rushing towards the last-mentioned figures, leaping over a fallen figure with a spear over his shoulder. A runner behind has seized the deer by the tail. Above is a figure on a horse riding towards the right; behind him a man with a sword or spear, and in front one with a halbert. To the right are one or two figures supplicating, one of them having a sword by his side. There are also two or three figures in the scene which are not clearly made out. To the right of it a tall figure is seen entering a doorway, and farther to the right is a large in-door scene. In the centre of this a rāja is seated on a throne; to the right of it stand two females, the second with the large oblong fan-like object remarked before. Below them and the throne five females are doing reverence or supplicating. To the left below, on a low seat, a stout man is addressing the rāja, and above him are nine other male faces, while four more—perhaps female slaves—appear behind the throne.

In the last scene to the right are three small, fat figures below, with poles over their shoulders and not touching the ground. On the pole and the head of one sit other two similar figures, one with a pole (perhaps a sword), and over their heads springs a man on horseback and another clinging to its tail.

Above is a long single-line inscription, but too much weatherworn, I fear, to be made anything of.

No. 189.

1 foot 3½ inches by about 10½ inches, and 2½ feet out of the earth. The east face of a pillar, the back split off and broken where the chamfering of the corners begins. The half disc on one face and most of the smaller ones on the sides are left.

On the face under the half disc is a scarcely-legible inscription in one and a half lines, in small characters, with very long stems.

No. 190.

This is a fine double disc lying just behind No. 194. On the face of it is a large dāgaba, filling nearly a third of the circle with the multiple umbrella ornament. Below are two kneeling worshippers, and on the left eight females paying reverence to it, one with a dish in her right hand. On the right are five men playing on musical instruments.

Nos. 191–194.

Nos. 191 and 193 are the lower portions of rail pillars, and Nos. 192 and 194 double discs. No. 191 has been much split and shattered in excavating. The back half disc is much decayed; the front one is also damaged.

Of No. 192, the front is split off and destroyed. On the upper left corner has been an inscription of which the syllables *(p)utakasa* only are left. The back disc is also much worn. No. 193 (see Plate XV*g*) in front of No. 189 has the lower disc almost entire; but above, the slab has been very much shattered and broken. In the middle compartment a rāṇī sat on a round-backed seat or throne, while a slave in front bathed or chafed her feet and a female stood on each side. In the compartment to the left a figure was coming out of a door; in that to the right a rāja was leaning against his horse.

No. 194 is much weatherworn in front. It has had an inscription on the upper right-hand corner, now rotted off except three letters—*sa* and *dāna*.

No. 62B.

From behind Nos. 192–195 I had several stones dug out; they were all broken fragments thrown in behind the rail, as if to give it support. Among them was a small standing figure of Buddha, the head gone and with a very faint inscription on the base.

No. 63B.

Also a very large fragment of a statue holding a flower in his hands, as if making an offering of it. A rich necklace of seven strings with a square clasp across it bearing, perhaps, a three-hooded cobra, falls down over his chest. His clothing is fixed by a belt round his waist, and is carefully depicted, both in front and on the back. Unfortunately both head and feet are gone. Fragments of a finely-carved rail pillar and disc, a piece of coping stone with a fragment of an inscription, &c., were also found.

No. 195.

About 2 feet 10 inches by 2 feet 9 inches. A fragment of a split coping stone. On the left is a *toraṇa* gateway of the Sanchi pattern, in front of which are two horses with plumes, and below are four men in earnest conversation. Above, to the right of the gateway, are the heads of a horse and of a large elephant, and to the right of the last is a tree, below which has been a tall figure (now broken off) with an umbrella. To the right again, are five tall figures (partly broken off) with Andhra headdresses.

Behind this stone is first an octagonal pillar, into the side of which No. 194 is mortised, 13 inches through or 8⅝ inches each side; and second a split portion of a pillar 1 foot 4 inches, by perhaps originally 1 foot. Into this latter No. 196 is mortised. Some other blocks have been piled up at the back of these.

No. 196.

This is a double disc, considerably injured in front and with an inscription on the upper left corner of the tenon—

chhadākichasa seṭhipamakhasa
bhadaniga[ma]sa suchi
dānaṁ.

"The pure gift of Chhadakicha (Chhandakṛitya) the chief of the merchants, the pious trader."—(Dr. Hultzsch.)

No. 197.

The lower portion of another rail pillar *in situ*, but very much injured in the excavation. It has been richly sculptured and carved on both sides.

No. 198.

7 feet 8 inches by 2 feet 6 inches. A rail pillar, complete on the back to the top of the central disc, except that one edge has been broken off. On the back, besides the discs, are three comical whimpering *gaṇa*. It lies on its face, the upper portion of which is split off to below the middle of the central disc. In what is left are several female figures in positions not easily accounted for. In the central area below it is a man moving, apparently in great haste, before whom a female kneels and supplicates: beyond her are three other figures, and another female is behind the man to the left. The right-side compartment is destroyed, except parts of three female figures. The left contains a man and woman on seats and five figures behind them, one (apparently a female) with a very peculiar turban or head-dress.

No. 199.

About 2 feet 7 inches square. A piece of coping stone, the front split off. Over the flower roll is seated, with hands joined, a *Nāgarāja* with a female *chauri*-bearer on each side. On the medallion upon the roll below is a star formed of four triśūlas.

No. 200.

This is a single disc of the rail, No. 39 pattern.

No. 201.

A broken fragment of coping stone, apparently a corner piece, with a margin up the left side, and a female (head gone) standing on a *makara*. Then a division cuts her off from the next piece, in which a man appears trying to escape from four women who hold him by the leg and arms. Above him, in another panel, have been other figures now broken off.

On the back is a throne with the *pāda* on it; probably the wheel has been above and two worshippers behind the throne. Below a double *makara* mouth forms a shield on the roll.

The upper part of this stone lies behind the pillars between Nos. 194 and 196, and below some others.

No. 202.

This is the lower right-hand fragment of a slab with a throne and footstool: a man and woman stand on the right of it and a *dēvata* flies above. The rest is gone.

No. 203.

This has been a double rail disc, but the front is split off.

No. 204.

4 feet 9 inches by 2 feet 7 inches. A fragment of the outer half of a coping stone. The area above the flower roll has the throne over the *pāda* and the wheel above, on the lion pillar, with two seated worshippers. On a medallion on the roll is a star made of four triśūlas.

No. 205.

This is a large fragment of a slab, on the lower half of which is Buddha seated and teaching, the foliage of a tree half surrounding the aureole (*bhāmandala*) behind his head. On his right a small figure is about to strike at him with a sword or club. On his left a similar figure makes a grimace with his hands joined, and behind him a female stands and touches Buddha's knee. Below the figure with the sword a man sits as if in contemplation, and above on each side is a *dēvata* with a dish filled with something.

Over this is an inscription in two lines rather faint, but which the enumerator has done his best to spoil by painting the number over it with thick tar.

Above this was another panel with the throne and footstool in the centre, and a deer and worshipper at each side, the rest broken away.

No. 64B.

Behind No. 206, but nearer to No. 197, at the foot of the brick parapet I found this stone, which is a fragment of a stone similar to No. 23B and Mr. Sewell's No. 52. In a narrow compartment on the left is a man standing with his left hand on his girdle. In the second compartment is Buddha standing preaching, two females kneel to him on the left, and another brings forward to him a boy on the right; behind her is another tall one, also with a boy, and behind are four other females and one male, while behind the two kneeling women on the left are two men.

Below in a recessed member are four harpy figures, and on the quadrantal moulding below is part of a half-obliterated inscription. It seems probable that Mr. Sewell's No. 61, which (with two others) seems to have been carried off by the Duke of Buckingham's party early in 1880, was a part of this stone. On the back are also harpy figures and some scratchings as if a design had been first begun on the back and then given up.

No. 206 (Sewell's No. 16).

15 feet 9 inches by 4 feet 7 inches by 10 inches. This is a very large slab, hewn only on one face, on which have been three ornamental pilasters (one of them quite hewn off). These pilasters can

No. 18 (Slab No. 65B)

No. 19 (Slab No. 69B)

No. 20 (Slab No. 71B)

No. 21 (Slab 210)

No. 22 (Slab No. 217)

No. 23 (Slab No. 78B)

No. 24 (Slab No. 222)

J. Burgess fecit

only be compared with those in the Vihâra at Pitalkhorâ and with those on the stûpa at Jaggayyapêṭa. The base consists of three thin plinths as in the Nâsik and other caves, supporting a thick *loṭa*-shaped body, carved with leaf and bead patterns. Over the lip of this stands a projecting member of about the same height with three *gaṇa* in the one case and two winged elephants in the other. On this stands the shaft with a central disc in the middle, and a half one above and below, the corners chamfered off between. Over this is the capital, exactly of the Pitalkhorâ type, then a line of beads and an abacus of three thin members, on which stand two winged animals (? horses and lions) supporting a quadrantal moulding. (See Plate XIV.)

Beyond this lie large fragments of at least seven great rail pillars of brown granite, hewn exceedingly smooth above the ground level, and each with a dark streak across, about the level of the middle of the lowest bar, possibly caused by water: the upper edge is sharply defined in all cases, and it wears off downwards in about 3 inches.

At the east gateway, where the stones have stood, the enumerator has omitted to number many important slabs.

No. 207.

18 inches by 18 inches by 3 feet. This is an octagonal pillar with a rail-pattern ornament round the base and a circular cap (broken) on the top, slightly hollowed above. It seems to have been a stand for something, but for what is hard to guess.

No. 65B.

Is a broken double rail disc. The back is pretty entire; but of the face only a fragment remains, with about a dozen heads in it with peculiarly varied head-dresses.

On the upper right corner is an entire inscription. (See Plate V, 18)—

Chetiavadakasa bha-
yaṁta Budhino bhâtu-
no u(? pa)pāno ā-
nugāmika
suchi dānaṁ.

No. 66B.

About 3 feet 9 inches by 2 feet 4 inches: a triangular fragment of a coping stone, which has been carved with unusual care.

On the left a portion of a tree is seen with fruit on it minutely carved, and among the foliage a head, perhaps of a child,—the rest is broken off. Below, two females stand in an attitude of supplication to it, and a third stoops down. To the right in an upper apartment a portly figure is seated, another bows to him, and beyond stand a young man with some round object in his right hand and a female with her hair knotted upon her shoulder.

In the area below is a lady and her maid supplicating a man who carries an infant in his arms. Below has been a lady seated in a chair and another behind her.

To the right of this are houses and a *champa* tree at the door of one of them. Above to the right is a *râja* seated on his throne and a man bringing in an infant. To the right of the throne a female stands with her hands crossed. Behind it are two heads and to the left other two looking out of a small apartment. Below this the stone is broken away, and to the right are left only the head of a man and woman. On the curve above is an inscription, (see Plate IV, 17) which Dr. Hultzsch reads—

niḷikā mahayāya Sujātaṁya mahâvesibhutāya duhutāya bhikhuniya Rohāya aṭhalokadhaṁmavitivatāya dā[*naṁ*].[1]

and translates,—

"The gift of the female mendicant Rohā who has passed beyond the eight worldly conditions, the daughter of the very venerable Sujāta who had been a great *vesi* (?) . . ."

---

[1] *Bhikhuniya* looks like *bhigu°*; *°loka°*; like *°leka°*; the *dha* of *dhaṁma* is scratched; the ī of *vitivatāya* may be short.—E.H.

No. 67B.

1 foot 5¼ inches by 1 foot 1 inch, and about 3½ feet above ground. The bottom of a pillar stuck obliquely in the ground with the greater part of a dāgaba in low relief on the east face.

No. 68B.

1 foot 8 inches by 1 foot, and about 9¼ feet long. Apparently one half of the lower portion of a pillar. About 3½ feet of it is undressed; over this is a dāgaba on the front, having a five-headed snake between two pilasters on the drum, and about 21 little umbrella-like flowers hung about the capital. Above this the pillar becomes octagonal, but is broken off about 1½ feet higher, through the middle of an inscription, which must have covered three faces.

We can only read—

Adha . pa . bha (?) . . . . .
tukasa dānama . . .
pasanikamātulena da

Many fragments of broken pillars and rails lie about here, with little bits of beautiful sculpture on them.

No. 208.

This is the lower portion of a rail pillar, the back peeled off, and only a good-sized portion of the lower half disc in front and the band below it left.

No. 69B.

A small fragment of stone stuck in the ground in front of the last; has the following fragment of an inscription (see Plate V, 19) in letters of the Mauryan type—

- *senagopasa Muḍukutalasa thabo.*

"A pillar of the general Muḍukuṭala."—(Dr. Hultzsch.)*

No. 70B.

4 feet 4 inches by 1 foot 7 inches by 11 inches. A little further to the right is a large piece of perfectly plain coping stone.

No. 71B.

About 2 feet broad by 3 feet 8 inches high. Behind the last is a fragment with part of a pilaster on it similar to those on No. 206, only it has been mostly knocked off. The animals over the capital were probably winged elephants. Above is a frieze, on the lower member of which is part of an inscription (see Plate V, 20) in Mauryan characters, reading—

Sidhaṁ Oḍiparivenene vāsikasa dhamakadhikasa Budhi . . .

"Success! [*The gift*] of the preacher Budhi, who resides in Oḍiparivenena."—(Dr. Hultzsch).

Above this is a slightly recessed flat member with upright oblong holes in it; then a fillet with a winged horse, a buffalo, an elephant, another winged horse, and a boar, each pursuing the other. On the frieze over this is neatly carved, in one compartment, the throne and tree behind it, with the *pāda* on the footstool and two men with flower vases. Next to this are three rail pillars with the discs between, all neatly ornamented. A narrow projecting member surmounts this. The upper part of the stone is only five or six inches thick, while below it is double as much.

No. 72B.

This is a small fragment, 2 feet broad, of a similar slab, stuck in the earth, very much abraded, and only a portion of the frieze left, with the wheel over the *pāda*, and these over two rings not observed elsewhere.

No. 209.

About 18 inches by 2 feet. A fragment with the base of a pilaster upon it, and below is a sort of dado, ornamented with geese carrying each a flower in its mouth.

This is lying loose on the ground near No. 214.

No. 73B.

In front of No. 208 is another piece of slab with the base of a pilaster in the corner of it upheld by a dwarf.

No. 210.

About 3 feet by 5 feet. Another slab of the same sort, the pilaster pretty entire except the base of it. The animals on the capital are winged lions. On the architrave is (see Plate V, 21)—

Sidhaṁ uwāsikaya Sivalāya saputikaya saduhutukāya deyadhaṁ[*maṁ*].

"Success! The meritorious gift of the female worshipper Sivalā (Śivalā), together with her sons, together with her daughters."—(Dr. Hultzsch).

The next member has four holes in it, as if for little wooden blocks to represent the ends of beams, and above it are ten animals, six of them with wings. In the frieze are the throne, *pāda* and tree, with two attendants bearing vases; and in another compartment the dāgaba and worshippers, the compartments being separated by pieces of ornamental rail pattern.

No. 74B.

About 3½ feet by 1 foot by 6 inches. A fragment like a piece of plain coping with part of a rather rudely-cut inscription reading—

Sanajanānasadati ? ?

No. 75B.

1 foot 10 inches by 2 feet by 2 inches. Two *pāda* with the shield between two *swastikas* on each heel, and two worshippers on each side. The front portion, where the inscription should be, is gone.

No. 211.

2 feet 11 inches by about 3 feet. This is the greater portion of one of the flower-vase slabs. It is broken across the bottom.

No. 212.

About 2 feet 11 inches broad by 2 feet 9 inches high. The lower portion of a slab, with Buddha seated preaching, having a Nāgarāja, his queen, and a *dēvata* on each side. The upper left-hand portion of this panel and the whole of the upper one is broken off.

No. 76B.

About 2 feet 2 inches by 2 feet 8 inches. The right-hand portion of a panel of a large slab: contains a dāgaba with worshipper and a *dēvata* to the right.

No. 213.

A large portion of a double disc.

No. 214.

2 feet 7 inches by about 4 feet by 6 inches high. A large slab, the upper part broken into four pieces but could be cemented. It has the wheel above and the tree below, each over the throne, and with two male worshippers and a *dēvata* on each side.

No. 215.

Is a small fragment from a similar panel containing a worshipper.

No. 77B.

Two pieces of other slabs, with three lions across the one, and two on the other.

No. 217.

A fragment of an inner rail pillar, smooth on both edges and with part of an inscription (see Plate V, 22) in the same characters as on No. 78B—

-isa atavāsikasa pavachi[*ta*] . . .

No. 78B.

Another fragment of what looks like part of a pillar of the inner rail lies between the upper end of No. 68B and No. 66B, on which is a portion of an inscription (see Plate V, 23) reading—

ye(?) *liyanaṁ mahavinayadharasa aya Budh-*

Taking this portion first and reading the part on No. 217 after it, Dr. Hultzsch renders the whole as—

"[The gift] of the ascetic . . . the disciple of the venerable Budhi . . who is very well versed in the *Vinaya*."[1]

No. 218.

2 feet 3 inches long and 6 inches thick. This is a stone very similar to No. 78B, and may be a part of the coping. The end of an inscription on it is in rather smaller and better-formed letters—

khapatino saputakasa dāna djvathapatha . . ?

No. 219.

The upper left corner of a slab with the wheel on it, like No. 214.

No. 220.

A fragment of another large thin slab, of a different pattern, having apparently had two or three smaller flower vases above, a band of flower pattern below them, and then animals.

No. 221.

Another slab, broken at the top and very like No. 214, only that there is a man and woman on each side the throne below the tree, and the positions of the worshippers in the upper panel are also different. There has been an inscription on the dividing belt, but it is entirely abraded, and the number is painted over it with tar.

No. 222.

5 feet 7 inches by 3 feet 2 inches. One of the most perfect of the larger slabs. On the upper panel is the wheel above the throne and two male worshippers seated on each side, with a *dēvata* above.

The lower panel has Buddha on a low seat, his feet not laid *over* one another as at Ajanṭa, &c., but one in front of the other. His left hand is held in front with the palm turned upwards, but the back does not rest on the foot; the right hand is held up as if in the act of addressing. The robe is full and loose, and a corner of it rests on the left shoulder. Behind the head is an aureole, and over (partly round) it, the foliage of a pipal tree. On each side are two male worshippers with the Andhra turban and two *dēvatas* above bringing presents.

---

[1] Compare *tripiṭakadhara* (Childers, s.v. *dharo*).

Up the right side of the slab is a border about 5 inches broad with six medallions on it; there is a good deal of lime up the left side and along the top of this slab.

On the lower edge of the slab is an inscription in three long lines, but it is a good deal peeled and chipped off, and of the last line probably nothing can be certainly made out. This inscription is of special interest as containing the name of the capital *Dhaṁñakaṭaka*. (See Plate V, 24.) I read it thus at first sight (there is a misspelling in *Bhagapato* for *Bhâgavato*)—

(1) *Sidhaṁ namo Bhagapato logatisa Dhaṁnakaṭakasa upāsakasa*
(2) *go-* (?) *pata sa . p . dharakhitasa gharaniya chapajumaya pusa cha haghasa Budhi*
(3) *budhi . . . . dharakhitasa sava . . . . .* ?

The word *Bhagavato*, it will be observed, is wrongly spelt; but the chief interest of this inscription is in the mention of the city of Dhanakaṭaka the capital of the Andhra kingdom and probably on the site of the modern Dharaṇikoṭa.

No. 223.

Is a very small fragment of the base of a rail pillar, with only a portion of the band under the lower half disc left on it.

No. 224.

2 feet 9 inches by 1 foot: this is a fragment similar to No. 216, which has been built in with lime in its present condition. It has two lions and a boar in line, and below a band of rudely-carved rail pattern.

No. 225.

This is a fragment forming the upper left corner of a slab of the same style as Nos. 16, 81, 115, 131, &c., only there are no holes for iron pins in the centres of the triśūla ornaments, of which one and a large piece of the second are left, also two of the animals on the band below and the flower-like umbrellas of the dāgaba that occupied the lower panel.

Nos. 226 and 227.

These are double discs of the outer rail, in pretty good preservation, but, like so many others, the central projecting circle is broken out, as it usually is in three instances out of the four.

No. 228.

Is another disc which has been much injured in excavating, the flanges and edges being broken off all round.

No. 229.

This is a rough block of stone with a rudely blocked-out figure of an animal on one side. It is of no interest.

No. 230.

A single disc of the outer rail, the centre broken out.

No. 231.

2 feet 10 inches by about 4 feet. This is a slab (the top broken off) of the same style as Nos. 72, 74, 120, 219, 221, 214: only the throne and *pāda* below it with the feet of the attendants are left of the upper panel. On the lower, is the tree over the throne, &c., a tall man on the left side holding up a banner in front of it, while the corresponding figure on the right holds up a double umbrella; each is attended by his wife worshipping, and above is a *dēvata* with gifts on each side.

Below is a two-line inscription, a good deal weatherworn and partly illegible, read doubtfully—

Sidhaṁ Saparatarabha . . . . pasa . . . .
-pa . . kasamahavi . . sa . . . . . saghasa . . . . .

No. 232.

3 feet by 4 feet 2 inches. This is the most perfect of the flower-vase slabs, Nos. 1, 22, 80, 104, 107, 117, 129 and 130, 211, 237, 252. It has a narrow projecting border up the right side, but none on the left or top. Lime along the top shows that it has been built in somewhere.

On the base is an inscription in one and a quarter lines of which a good deal is legible. (See Plate VI, 25.) Dr. Hultzsch reads it from my impression,—

Sidhaṁ Chaṁmākārasa Nāgagha [rutapa] putasa Vidhikasa samatukasa sabhayakasa sabhatukasa putasa cha Nagasa sama[dhu [1]]tukasa sanātimitabaṁdhavasa deyadhaṁma.

His translation is,—

"Success! A tablet on which is a brimming jar,[2] the meritorious gift of the shoemaker Vidhika, the son of Nāgagharutapa (?) with his mother, with his wife, with his brothers; and of his son Nāga, together with his daughters, with his relations, friends, and connections."

No. 233.

Beside the preceding lies the fragment of the base of a similar slab.

No. 79B.

2 feet 6 inches by 1 foot 5½ inches by 8 inches. In front of the last, in the trench, lies a coping stone entire but perfectly plain, with mortise hole below and rounded top. It has a slight curve.

No. 234.

1 foot 5 inches by 1 foot. This is a roughly-carved dāgaba with a worshipper to the left of it. It appears to have been the corner of a large slab, but in its present form it has been built in with lime.

No. 235.

15 inches by 20 inches. The upper right-hand corner of a slab like No. 231.

No. 236.

The upper right-hand corner of a slab like Nos. 232 and 237.

No. 237.

A slab quite similar to No. 232, but broken slantly across the upper part and all the upper right-hand parts gone.

No. 238.

A small fragment with a lion on it, and sticking to bricks and lime at the back.

No. 239.

The head of a figure with small curls all over the scalp and a round *tilaka* on the forehead.

Nos. 240 and 241.

Two pieces of split coping stone with the roll upborne by men.

No. 242.

2 feet 2 inches by 11 inches by 5½ inches. A piece of a small coping stone, the ends only broken off, perfectly plain.

---

[1] This letter is an addition, and is entered below the line.

[2] A brimming jar is considered a lucky emblem, see Childers, *s.v. puṇṇo*.

No. 25 (Slab No. 232)

No. 26

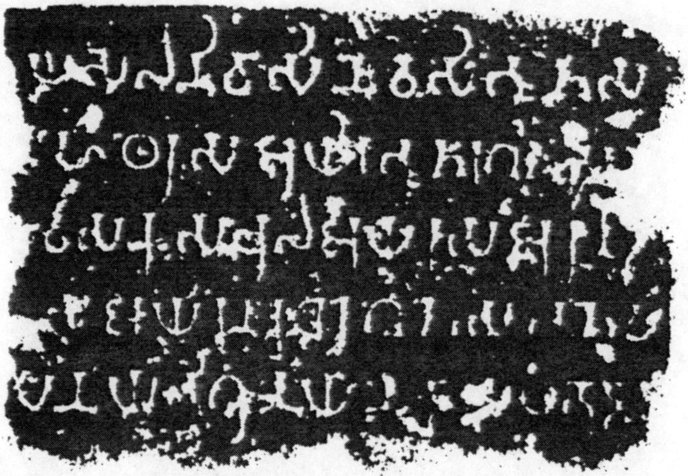

No. 27 (Sewell's No. 17. See text P. [illegible])

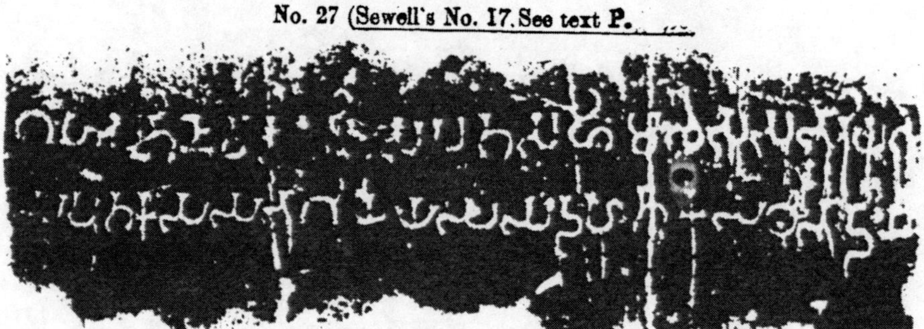

No. 28 (Sewell's No. 89. See text P. 51)

J. Burgess fecit

No. 243.

Another fragment like No. 238, with a lion.

No. 244.

A small fragment that looks like part of an octagonal pillar, with chaitya window pattern on one side.

No. 245.

Another small fragment of one of the large thin slabs, with only the body of a female worshipping on it.

No. 246.

A double disc, the centres entire, but the upper side much chipped and broken in excavating.

No. 247.

A split fragment of the outer rail, with a very tall pillar-like dāgaba or rather tower, for it has not the usual capital and no *chhatri*; it is attended by two figures in long flowing locks.

Nos. 248 and 250.

Two fine well-cut double discs, in fair preservation.

No. 249.

About 15 inches by 10 inches: the left-hand portion of the base of a slab similar to No. 232. It has had an inscription in two long lines, much weatherworn and most of it wanting. It begins—

Sidhaṁ Namo Bhagavato Haṁghi[*gapa*]*tiputasa*[1] *Dusika* [*sa*]
saputakasa saduhutukasa sanati[*m*]*itabaṁdhava*[*sa*] . . .

"Success! Adoration to the holy one! [*The gift*] of Dusika, the son of the householder (?) Haṁghi, together with his sons, with his daughters, with his relations, friends, and connections . . ."—(Dr. Hultzsch).

No. 252 is perhaps another fragment of the same slab.

No. 251.

It is a pity this curious double disc has been so broken. It has been full of figures. In a compartment at the top is a man on a couch to which another is approaching with a long sword, as if to murder him. Behind are other two figures. To the right is a round thatched hut, a doorway and trees; but the lower portion of the slab is broken away.

On the left portion a male figure is seated in the middle addressed by two in front, while behind and in front of him are numerous females with the round *tilaka* on the forehead.

No. 252.—See No. 249.

No. 253.

This is the lower portion of one of the slabs with a dāgaba on the lower panel. This has one worshipper and a *dēvata* on each side.

It is to be remarked that all the slabs bearing the flower vase, wheel and tree, wheel and dāgaba, *triśūla* and dāgaba, have a more weatherworn appearance than any others. A majority also have had inscriptions. They would seem, therefore, to have been in prominent and exposed positions without much shelter from the weather.

---

[1] *Haṁghi°* or *Paṁghi°*; perhaps *gahapati* is meant.

No. 254.

Apparently a portion of the top of No. 1.

No. 255.

A piece of a split coping stone, with the flower roll upheld by a man. The top, as in many similar cases, has been hewn off; and here iron pegs have been inserted at distances of a foot apart along the upper margin.

No. 80B.

At the south gate I turned up a sort of step and found it to be the base of a pillar similar to No. 3, but with no carving but the half discs.

No. 81B.

2 feet 4 inches by 11½ inches by 5 inches. A stone with a curve on the plane of its face, carved on the upper surface with men and animals, all much worn, as if it had been long used as a step, of which it probably originally formed part.

At the end of and inside No. 4, built in with bricks and mud, were eight or nine pieces, five of them being parts of a beautifully-carved pillar, a piece of railing, and other stones.

No. 82B.

The five pieces of the pillar alluded to fit together, and it is possible more of it may turn up on further excavation. One piece is the right side of the lower half disc, the corner over which is filled in with a beautiful honeysuckle pattern preserved on a second fragment. Two fragments of the band below the central disc show a man in the central compartment moving violently to the right; a figure kneels before him with a triple-hooded snake by his side, and above or behind him is a figure with the right hand uplifted and with a rod or staff, and carrying some object over his shoulder in the left.

In the right-hand panel on the extreme right is Buddha holding out his alms-bowl. A man with a *jaṭa* head-dress, a scanty cloth over his shoulders, and his left foot on a lotus is about to place something in the alms-bowl, while a female behind him is joining her hands in reverence. A fourth figure behind Buddha is destroyed, except the right foot.

Of the central panel only one fragment remains, containing parts of some worshippers.

No. 83B.

In front of Nos. 10 and 11 I dug out the upper portion of a narrow pillar much chipped and damaged, but with a few letters of an early inscription above the upper half disc.

No. 84B.

This broken slab was found near No. 64B, and has evidently formed part of the same frieze, and is of about the same size, broken also along the right end. It is a good deal weatherworn. The principal figure is Buddha with *nimbus*, standing under a tree with a figure kneeling on his left and another paying respect; to the left of these are two females, one with high head-dress and something like the foliage of a tree behind the head of each; a third kneels in the lower left corner, and five beyond form an audience. On Buddha's left are apparently two disciples, a child or monkey, and five other figures, one above the rest being a female. In the upper right side is a balcony with three apertures and five figures looking out from them. Below have been the harpy figures and a quadrantal moulding.

No. 85B.

This is a small fragment found in the south-south-west, with Buddha seated, his legs crossed under him and preaching; an attendant on each side are now represented only by their heads; and below are two worshippers with high turbans kneeling over the footstool.

No. 29 (Slab No. 88B)

J. Burgess fecit

No. 86B.

This is also a portion of a small slab with a dāgaba in the centre, with *chhatris* over it, and a figure (perhaps a female) standing in a *toraṇa* gate on the left side : the right is broken off.

No. 87B.

A small fragment from the south-west side, containing part of the capital of a small pilaster carved on a slab. It has two lions over the abacus, and the representation of the end of a bracket resting on them. Over this are carved the members of an architrave.

No. 88B.

On moving 146, a circular slab 2 feet 1 inch in diameter was found with a mortise hole in the centre surrounded by a lotus, and this again by a sunk area carved with rays. The outer border is raised and has a well-cut inscription which leaves no doubt that these stones were *chhatras* over dāgabas. The largest is that at the well, 4 feet 9 inches in diameter.

The inscription round this (see Plate VII, 29) reads—

Uvāsikāya cha Dayabudhiṇo mātuya saputikāya sadutukāya airānantaye pabhāhina chediyasa chhata deya dhamaṁ.

No. 89B.

In removing the base of No. 142, I found it propped behind by four fragments of a broken pillar. Two of them belong to the left side of the space over the central circle. On a throne is a rāja seated, with his queen on his right hand, her right foot on a square footstool, and a female fitting on her anklets. Beside her sits a monkey looking on. To the right a man sits on his knees with short curly hair and holding up a platter with a cobra on it. At this the rāja and his queen are looking. Over his head is the foliage of a tree. To the right of the throne a female sits resting her head upon the back of her right hand, which lies on the corner of the back of the throne. Behind her is another with some large object on a platter, and to the left are two others; their heads are on the third fragment, which contains the edge of the upper half disc. The fourth piece is the end of the upper border and contains a dwarf, apparently feeding an animal with branched horns, and a broad face; in front of it is another, of which the head is gone.

The sharpness with which these fragments are carved increases the regret that such sculptures have been so destroyed. It is probable that a thorough excavation round the line of the outer rail would bring to light many beautiful fragments.

No. 90B.

This is a triangular fragment, which perhaps belongs to the coping at the eastern gate, where sculpture of similar character was found.

STONES EXCAVATED BY MR. SEWELL.

The stones excavated by Mr. Sewell and left where he found them have been described among those enumerated on the survey plan. His numbers have mostly been washed off. But a large number of stones, evidently not *in situ* where he found them he judiciously removed to a small shed built on the north side of the excavation. Mr. Sewell's accounts of these stones in his report are generally accurate, and therefore a fresh description of them in detail is not necessary. In the shed are his numbers 1, 2, 5, 9, 12, 14, 17, 18, 21, 22, 23, 29, 32, 38, 47, 48, 49, 50, 51, 52, 53, 54, 55, 56, 58, 59, 60 (61 wanting), 62–73, 76 and 86.

No. 61, described by Mr. Sewell as a small stone with a portion of an inscription on it, and which most probably formed part of that on another stone, cannot now be found. This and one or two others from the circle were carried off, I am informed, by the Duke of Buckingham and suite.

No. 17. This pillar, fully 8 feet long by 4 feet 4 inches in periphery, has a fragment left of a rectangular base 13½ inches by 17½ inches, above which it changes into an irregular octagon. It bears part of a long Sanskrit inscription, each line of which breaks off incomplete, as if it had been continued on an adjoining slab or pillar. This was probably the shaft of a pillar whose base (No. 67B) is still near the east gateway, together with part of the base of another similar (but probably thicker) pillar (No. 68B), on the upper portion of which may have been the remainder of this inscription. It is a record of the Pallavas and contained a long dynastic list, in which Mr. Fleet reads the names of the following Pallava kings :—

Siṁhavarmā.	Siṁhavarmā II.	Mahēndravarmā.
Siṁhavishṇu.	Arkavarmā.	Sūra.
Nandivarmā.	Ugravarmā.	Pallava.

It is probably of much the same date as that published in the *Indian Antiquary*, Vol. VIII, page 273, which also mentions a Siṁhavishṇu and a Mahēndravarmā, then Narasiṁhavarmā, Mahēndravarmā II, Paramēśvaravarmā, Narasiṁhavarmā II, Paramēśvaravarmā II, Nandivarmā, Pallavamalla-Nandivarmā.

On the other side is a Pāli inscription in two lines (see Plate VI, 27) reading—

Gahapatino Vāsumitasaputasa Himalasa sabhāriyasa
Saputakasa sabhagineyasa saduhutukasa thabho dānaṁ.

"The gift of a pillar from the householder Himala, the son of Vāsumitra, with his wife, his sons, his sister's sons, and his daughters."

The "flourishy scroll" which Mr. Sewell mentions as above the Pāli inscription seems to be a mediæval form of the syllable *Śrī* multiplied several times downwards. The "roughly-cut triple umbrella" on the base is what remains of a group of umbrellas. Compare No. 68B.

No. 18 is outside at the end of the shed, and seems to have been well pounded with stones thrown at it since Mr. Sewell left it. There are a few letters of an inscription on the inner face of it, but so weatherworn as to be scarcely legible.

No. 29 is a portion of one of the large slabs described above under Nos. 16, 30B, 115, 131, 225.

In his account of No. 32 Mr. Sewell has mixed up the account of two stones which he has numbered "32." The one, a small fragment with a figure of rāja with suppliants on each side; the other, the lower right corner of a flower-vase slab with the ends of three lines of inscription on it.

No. 47 has fragments of an inscription on it. This and Nos. 48, 49, 50, 51 are all similar to those described above as Nos. 10B, 11B, and 12B.

His No. 52 is an exceedingly beautiful slab and is only matched by No. 23B above described.

No. 67 is a portion of the base of a flower-vase slab with a few letters of an inscription in two lines.

No. 69 is an interesting slab presenting, perhaps, a version of the *Chhadanta Jātaka*; the man carrying "two loads" is quite the counterpart of the huntsman in the Ajantā representation of the scene, and he carries four elephant-tusks on a *kāvaḍi*. He is also represented here beneath the great elephant as in the *Jātaka* story, and again as sawing off his tusks.

Nos. 70, 71 and 72 are at Amarāvati and are to be removed to Madras along with many others for safety.

No. 71. It is hardly accurate to describe this as "one of the inner enclosure pillars." It must have been a pilaster employed in a specially prominent position. It has no mortises for the bars as the pillars have, and is sculptured. At the bottom is the throne with the *pāda* or footprints below it, and over it rises a pillar with the shaft richly ornamented in bands, in three main sections, at the top of each are three *gaṇa* or lions, and on the abacus two couchant lions with riders, above which is the *dharmachakra*. Two figures on lions form struts to the abacus of the capital, and on each side are pairs of worshippers floating in air—divine, human, and *nāga*.

No. 72 is the upper portion of a narrower slab of the same description, but with only one worshipper on each side in each tier, and without the lion-riders as struts.

No. 73. I am not quite decided about this being a head of Buddha. The *tilaka* on the forehead is not a usual feature in the statues of the Muni, and the ears are little longer than the natural size, while Buddha's are always elongated downwards.

On No. 76 is a portion of an inscription in large letters which have been cut through when the stone was applied to some other than its original purpose.

There is still one stone standing in front of the shed which deserves notice. No. 89 is a piece of coping stone of the outer rail, 2 feet 11 inches by 2 feet 8 inches by 1 foot, having on the outer side over the "roll" three *gaṇa* (much defaced) upholding a platform, from which the foreparts of three lions spring. On the inner side has been an animated scene, much defaced by exposure and ill-usage. On the left, below, is a house with an arched roof. Over it is a tree or shrub and two vessels at the side of a circular hut or house, which a man with a large bundle on his back is leaving and who is met by a man and woman, while behind him is seen the head of a third person. Behind and above all these is a long arched-roofed house, and above and beyond it are two horsemen going in opposite directions; to the right a footman running, and a third horseman before him. Beyond these last two is a wall over which two people look, and within it is a long figure, like Buddha, on a bier or couch, with a female at the head and three other figures beyond it. Below, or in the foreground, is a man running over rocks, looking back towards a tall figure leaning against the end of the conventional representation of the rocks. On the round of the top of the stone is part of an inscription (see Plate VI, 28) containing the name of king Sivama, and reading—

Rāño Siri Sivamakasadasapaniyagharikasaha . . . .

From the entrance of the village temple I removed also to the shed three fragments described by Mr. Sewell as Nos. 87 and 88.

I examined some of the stones at the well from which Mr. Sewell says he got his Nos. 70–72, but with the exception of a circular stone *chhatra*—4 feet 9 inches in diameter, I could not easily obtain access to any that were carved. The circular slab is carved as one of the wheel emblems and has a mortise hole in the centre for a shaft to uphold it as an umbrella, while the outside is polished.

The threshold of one of the temples outside the large one in the village is formed of a slab from the stūpa, and bears an inscription (see Plate VI, No. 26). In the walls of the same temple are many other slabs from the stūpa.

STONES AT BEZWĀḌA.

From Masulipatam there were removed to Bezwāḍa two large and five smaller pieces, of which the following very brief notes may suffice for the present:—

No. 1 is a small fragment much worn.

No. 2 has a female and parts of other figures on it.

No. 3 is a part of an archaic dāgaba with snakes round it.

No. 4, the largest, is a magnificent slab, the most perfect of all the dāgaba ones, with narrow ornamental pillars at each side and a frieze above full of figures. Buddha in the centre, his throne upheld by *gaṇa*, two females and other figures on his left, one tall male with club and other figures on his right; perhaps the whole is a version of the temptation. On each side three knobs (one on the right cut away by a hole), then a *nāga* and *nagini*; then three more knobs, the middle one in every case with a sculpture on it. Then on the left a tree (*pipal*) over a throne with feet and *dharma* symbol worshipped by twenty-two figures; behind this three knobs. On the right is the throne and cushions, and sixteen females mostly, if not all, asleep.

Under the frieze is an inscription much broken in the centre.

No. 5 is the lower portion of a dāgaba.

No. 6. A pillar carved on both sides, the top much damaged. The large disc has Buddha on the *Siṁhāsana*, with a tree (*pipal*) behind and nineteen figures round. Below are three compartments filled with figures, almost all perfect. Below this a lotus disc and belt of lions and foliage. On the back is a round disc upheld by three *gaṇa* with a two-third disc over a belt of deer, elephant, *makara*, &c., and foliage.

No. 7 is the horse under a chhatra coming out of a door, two figures before, an attendant and two dēvatas flying above.

The following is a list of the stones now at Amarāvati and Bezwāḍa:—

Statistics.

Stones enumerated in the Collector's report	255
Added or excavated since—Series B	90
Described in Mr. Sewell's report, not included above	44
Bezwāḍa stones described by Mr. Sewell	22
Slabs from Masulipatam	7
Total ..	418

The excavations of 1880 have laid bare the fragments that remain of the great procession path, which is pretty entire round nearly half the circle, and can be distinctly traced round the quadrant between the east and north entrances. In the fourth quadrant between east and south, which was excavated in Colonel Mackenzie's time, scarcely a trace is left, nor a fragment of any of the beautifully-carved slabs he indicated in his first rough plan, published by Mr. Sewell in his *Report*. Some of these slabs he probably removed himself; but the majority were either burnt into lime or carried off for other purposes; and the whole circle seems to have been plundered at different times, leaving not a single upright of the outer rail now entire. Both on the north-east and south-west, where the destruction seems to be most recent, there is a low brick base covered with plaster built up against the bottom of the pillars, about 20 inches high and 2 feet broad at the bottom, and rising in a sort of quadrantal curve against the pillars. In the south-west is also a fragment of a similar work of smaller dimensions for the support of the slabs of the inner rail, and near the end of it are the bases of four slabs still *in situ* (one of them a pilaster), their faces turned towards the procession path. At the back of these slabs is the base of a brick wall, about 2 feet thick, formed of very large bricks, and wherever several layers of bricks remain undisturbed, this wall shows a smooth face to the inside of the circle. Moreover, both at the south and west gates there are evidences that there were entrances into the inner area. The steps in these cases are of the same very large bricks as the circle, quite different in texture and size from any of those used in every other part of the excavation. There has probably been a similar entrance at the north, but it has been destroyed. These facts are against Mr. Sewell's theory of the whole area being filled by a gigantic stūpa.

The remains of a wall mentioned by Colonel Mackenzie in the south-to-west quadrant I sought for, but failed to find any trace of it, though, perhaps, the bricks were carried off soon after his time. But the plan on which this is marked is so inaccurate and so inferior in every respect to the one he afterwards prepared, and which is published in Mr. Fergusson's *Tree and Serpent Worship*, that it hardly deserves much attention. A wall 8 feet thick certainly deserved remark: may it not have been that part of it was 8 feet high? or did he mistake a short return inwards at the south gate of the wall supporting the inner rail and filled up behind with earth and brick *débris*, for a solid mass of the size he indicates?

It is noteworthy that wherever one digs at the back of the outer rail, broken slabs, statues, &c., are found jammed in behind it. The dark slate slabs too of the procession path are laid on a sort of concrete formed of marble chips, broken slabs, pillars, &c., as if it were, in its present form, a part of the work of reconstruction executed centuries later than the original.

It should also be remarked that to the south of the east gate are the lower halves of several very massive granite pillars which have formed part of the outer rail. They have been hewn and polished perfectly smooth, have stood closer together than the marble pillars, and have been connected by plain lenticular bars of marble of no great weight. Should we attribute these granite pillars to the period of reconstruction, or do they belong to the first erection?

ADDITIONAL NOTES ON THE ABOVE.

Since the above was printed off Dr. E. Hultzsch has sent me the following additional translations of inscriptions:—

Slab No. 8 (pp. 7, 8).

The inscription runs thus;—

[1] *Sidhaṁ Namo Bhagavato achar*[*iyana*]
[2] *mahavanasaliyāna Sāripu*[tāna a-]
[3] *malāna sisihasa Sagharu* . . . .[1]
[4] *gahagujā Kaṁḍasa Dhaṁm*[i] *lavāni-*
[5] *yaputasa gadhikasa vāniyasa*. .
[6] . . *bhasa sapitukasa samātuka*[sa sa]-
[7] *bha*[ri]*yakasa sabhatukasa sa*. . . .
[8] *saputakasa sadhutukasa sagha*[rasa]
[9] *sanatukasa sanatimitabaṁdhava*[sa]
[10] *saghadeyadhaṁmaṁ padhānama*[ḍa]*vo*
[11] *patiṭhav*[i]*to.*

---

[1] The construction of the first three lines is somewhat conjectural. Perhaps *sisiyasa* (*śishyasya*) should be read in line 3. The syllables *sa sanatuka* are repeated between lines 8 and 9.

Translation.

"Success! Adoration to the Holy One! A chief (?) pavilion (*pradhânamaṇḍapa*) has been established, the meritorious gift to the community (*saṁgha*) of the merchant Kaṁḍa, a perfumer (*gandhika*), the son of the merchant Dhamm[i]la (Dharmila),[1] from Sagharu .. *gahaguja* (?), the disciple of the pure teacher Sâriputa (Śâriputra) who lives in the hall in the great forest[2] .... together with his father, together with his mother, together with his wife, together with his brothers, together with [*his sisters*], together with his sons, together with his daughters, together with his house (?), together with his grandsons, together with his relations, friends and connexions."

No. 11B (p. 12).

Dr. Hultzsch reads the inscription thus;—

....[*ante*] *vasikâsa maheṁkhânâjakâsa bhâyaṁtâ Nâdhasirisa siso bhâyaṁtâ Bu* ....

"The venerable Bu ....., the disciple of the venerable Nâdhasiri (Nâthaśrî), the Maheṁkhânâjaka (?), the disciple of ...."

No. 36 (p. 16).

The following is Dr. Hultzsch's rendering of the inscription :—

....[*A*]*ya Kamâya Sa*[*dhugava*]
siniyâ dâna.

"The gift of the venerable Kamâ (*Kâmâ*) who resides at Sa[dhuga]."

No. 25B (p. 17).

The inscription, in late characters, runs:—

....[*gha*]*ṁpuṭâru ṭhâpitô cha* ....

No. 26B (p. 17).

For "some letters of an inscription," *read* "part of an inscription." Dr. Hultzsch reads it as follows :—

.... *satamasa naravasabhasaṁm*[*â*]*saṁbudhâdichasa* ‖ *saghakasa nârasalasa vâṇiyasa Nâgatisasa ghar-aṇiya Nâkhâya saha âpano putehi Haṁghikena Budhinâ Mûlena*.....

"(*Adoration*) to the truly enlightened Sun, the chief of men (*naravṛishabha*[3]), the best .... ‖ (*The gift*) of Nâkhâ, the wife of the merchant Nâgatisa (Nâgatishya), a member of the community (*saṁgha*), a *Nârasala* (?), together with her sons Haṁghika, Budhi, Mûla...."

No. 60 (pp. 18, 19).

The correct transliteration of the inscription is,—

budhara
jidâ.

No. 46B (p. 23).

The four lines of writing are in unintelligible Sanskṛit. Dr. Hultzsch writes: "Its purport seems to be that a Vaiśya, who receives sundry laudatory epithets, makes his obeisance to Buddha."

---

[1] Compare *Sapila* (Sarpila) in the Kuḍâ inscriptions.
[2] Compare the inscription on No. 231.
[3] The synonym *narâsabha* (*nararshabha*) is an epithet of Buddha according to Childers.—E.H.

No. 185 (p. 37).

The inscription reads :—

..... *chi kāya samanikiya*
..... (*ya*) *sabhaginikāya*
dāna.

"The gift of the female ascetic (*śramaṇikī*) ... together with her sisters."—(*Dr. Hultzsch.*)

No. 189 (p. 38).

Dr. Hultzsch reads the inscription thus :—

[1] [Ha]*ralūre Rāhulagahapatisa bhāriyāya* [Nā]*gīya* [b]*āl*[i]*kāya*
[2] [Dhaṁ]*māya natukānam* [dāna] *khaṁbo.*

"A pillar (*the gift*) of the grandsons of [Dhaṁ]mā (Dharmā), the daughter of [Nā]gī, (*and*) wife of the householder Rāhula in [Ha]ralūra."

No. 205 (p. 40).

Dr. Hultzsch thus reads the inscription, which is much injured.

[1] *Siddhaṁ Kutaparavane vathavaya pavajitikaya Sagharakhitāya bā*[li]*kaya ja*
[2] *pavajitikāya Hi*[ḷa]*ya Rumārikāya ja*[Se]*vayadā*[na deya] *dhaṁ*[mā] *upaṭā*

For *Kuta*°- we might however read *Deva*°- or *Jeta*°- ; and in the second line we should either have *udhapaṭā*, or *upaṭā* (= *utpaṭṭa*), which is a synonym of *udhapaṭā*.

Translation.

"Success! *Ūrdhvapaṭṭas*, meritorious gifts, the gift of the female ascetic Sagharakhitā (Saṁgharakshitā) who resides in Kutaparavana, and of (*her*) daughter, the female ascetic Hi[ḷā ?] and of her daughter [Se]vā."

No. 68B (p. 42).

The inscription is beautifully carved. It runs thus :—

Adhahabha ....
tukasa dāna ma ......
pasanikamātulena da. .

The only complete words are *dāna*, "gift," and *mātulena*, "by the maternal uncle."—(*Dr. Hultzsch.*)

No. 222 (pp. 44, 45).

The inscription (Plate V, No. 24) is read by Dr. Hultzsch and translated thus :—

[1] *Sidham*|| *Namo Bhagapato logātichasa* [1] *Dhaṁñakaṭakāsa upāsakasa*
[2] *Goṁdiputasa Budharakhitasa gharaniyacha Padumāya pusacha* [2] *Haṁghasa Budhi*...
[3] *Bodhi*..........*Budharakhitasa savaka*[sa]...[u]*dhapaṭā* [vasa]...

Translation.

"Success! Adoration to the Holy One, the Sun of the world (*lokāditya*)! *Ūrdhvapaṭṭas* (*the gift*) of the worshipper Buddharakhita of Dhaṁñakaṭa, the son of Goṁdī, and of (*his*) wife Paduma (Padma), and of (*their*) son Haṁgha...of the pious disciple (*śrāvaka* [3]) Budharakhita..."

---

[1] The *cha* has dropped out of this word (at p. 45) in the press; it was correctly given in my manuscript.
[2] In line 2 *pusa* looks like *ghusa* ; read *putasa*.
[3] See Childers, s.v. *sāvako*.

No. 231 (p. 45).

The inscription on this slab should read thus :—

[1] *Sidhaṁ Saṁyutakabhatukāna Pusaku*[dasa si]*sāna mahath*[e]*rana* [Ghuvanuvāna] *charanagata-atavāsikasa.*

[2] *Peṁḍapātikasa mahavanasalavathavasa Pasamasa Haṁghasa cha deyadhaṁma ima udhapa*[ṭo].

"Success! This *ūrdhvapaṭṭa* [1] (*is*) the meritorious gift of the mendicant (piṇḍapātika) Pasama (Praśama), who resides in the hall in the great forest (*mahāvanaśālā*), the disciple gone at the feet of the great Sthavira... the brother of Saṁyutaka (Saṁyuktaka) (*and*) disciple of Pusaku[da] (?), and (*the gift*) of Haṁgha."—(*Dr. Hultzsch.*)

No. 88B (p. 49).

The inscription (Plate VII, No. 29) from the stone *chhattra* is thus read and translated :—

Uvāsikiya chadaya Budhiṇo mātuya saputikāya sadutukāya airāna Utayipabhāhina chediyasa chhata deyadhamaṁ.

Translation.

"An umbrella (*chhattra*), a meritorious gift to the Chaitya (?) of the venerable Utayipabhāhins [2] by the female worshipper Chadā (Chandrā), the mother of Budhi, together with her sons, together with her daughters."

Inscription at the temple. (P. 51, line 16. Plate VI, No. 26.)

The inscription reads :—

[1] *yaselanivāsino Vasibhūtisa*
[2] [Ma]*hatherasa ayira Bhutarakhitasa*[a-]
[3] [te]*vāsikasa chula ayirasa ara*[ha-]
[4] [tasa] *ayira Budharakhitasa ate*[vā-]
[5] [si]*niya bhikhuniyā Na*[dāya] *thambo dā*[naṁ].

Translation.

"A pillar, the gift of Vasibhūti (Vasubhūti?) a resident in .. yasela, the disciple of the great *Sthavira*, the venerable Bhūtirakhita (Bhūtarakshita), (*and the gift*) of the female ascetic Na[dā] (Nandā), the female disciple of the venerable Budharakhita, the younger brother [3] of the venerable *Arhat.*"

JAGGAYYAPEṬA STŪPA.

Reference has been several times made above to the Stūpa near Jaggayyapeṭa, 30 miles north-west from Amarāvatī, which I excavated early in March. It was about 63 feet in diameter, but all the slabs had been carried off except those surrounding the basement of the dāgaba. These were generally quite plain with a pilaster up the edge similar to those described above on slab No. 206, but on a few there were carvings in very low relief and of an archaic type and of these one of the most perfect, found lying on its face, at the north gateway is represented on plate xvii. Some letters on other slabs are of the Maurya type and must date about 200 to 170 B.C. At the gates were tall pillars, and on portions of three of those from the east gate there was an inscription dated in the 20th year of Purushadatta, the son of the Māḍharī mother. The characters of these inscriptions belong to about 200 A.D.

The first found of the three was broken into three pieces and portions of it were wanting; the second I found in the roof of a ruined temple near the foot of the hill; and the third and most legible version on a pillar buried in the debris on the east side of the Dāgaba. Paṇḍit Bhagwānlāl Indrajī, who has prepared the following transcript, points out that all three are very nearly alike, but the first

---

[1] A slab bearing a flower-vase.—J.B.

[2] *Utayipabhāhin* seems to be the name of a School like *Dharmottarīya* (see No. 121, p. 27). Perhaps *utara* (= *uttara*) is to be read for *utayi*, and *pabhāhin* = *prabhāsin*. *Chediyasa* might mean "of a native of Chedi," but the construction would not be quite clear.

[3] See Childers, s.v. *cullo*.

has *gāme* more and reads *Kamākaraḍē gāmē Nacha(? ḍa)nūrē*, where the second and third have only *Kamākaraḍē Nada(?)nūrē*; and the second has *Bhagavato Budhasa puvadārē*, but the first and third *Bhagavato Budhasa Mahāchetiye puvadārē*, "at the eastern gate of the great Chaitya of Bhagawān Buddha."

Transcript.[1]

(1) *Sidhaṁ raño Māḍhariputasa Ikhākuṇaṁ Siri-vira-Purisadatasa savachharaṁ* 20 *vāsāpakham* 6 *divasa*
(2) 10 *Kamākaraṭhe Naḍanure vāthavasa āve*[*sa*]*nisa Nākachaṁdasaputro gāme Mahākādurūre āvesani—*
(3) *Sidhatho āpaṇo mātaraṁ Nāgilani*[*ṁ*]*purato katunaṁ gharaṇiṁ cha samudaniṁ bālakaṁ cha mulasiri*[*ṁ*]
(4) *bālikāṁ cha Nākabudhanikāṁ bhātukaṁ cha Budhinakaṁ tasa gharaniṁ Chakanikāṁ*[2] *bālakā che Nāgasiri Chaṁda—*
(5) *Siri bālikāya Sa*(*Si*)*dhathanika evam nāti-mita-saṁbadhivagena saha gāme Velagiriyaṁ Bhagavato*
(6) *Budhasa Mahāchetiya pubadāre ayaka-khaṁbe* 5 *save niyute apaṇo deyadhamaṁ savasatānaṁ hitasukhāya patithapita ti*||

This the Paṇḍit renders thus into Sanskṛit and English :—

Siddham. Rājño Māḍhariputrasyekshvākuṇāṁ vīra-Purushadattasya saṁvatsaraḥ 20 varshāpakshaḥ 6 divasaḥ 10 Kamākarāshtra-grāmē Naḍanūrē vāstavyāvēśanino Nāgachandrasya putro grāmē Mahākādurūre vāstavya āvēśani-Siddhārthas ātmano mātaraṁ Nāgilanīṁ purataḥ kṛitvā gṛihiṇīṁcha Samudriṇīṁ bālakaṁ cha Mūlaśriyaṁ bālikāṁ cha Nāgabudhnikāṁ bhrātrikaṁ cha Buddhinakaṁ tasya gṛihiṇīṁ Chakriṇikāṁ bālakau cha Nāgaśrī-Chandraśriyau bālikāṁ cha Siddhārthanikāṁ | Evaṁ jñāti-mitra-sambandhivargēṇa saha[tena] grāmē Vellagirau Bhagavato Buddhasya mahāchaityē pūrvadvārē āryakastambhāḥ paṁcha 5 sarvē niyuktāḥ | ātmano deyadharmaḥ sarvasatvānāṁ hitasukhāya pratishṭhāpita iti.

Translation.

To the perfect one[3]! On the 10th day of the 6th fortnight of the rainy season of Samvat 20 of the king, the illustrious Purisadata (Purushadatta), son of Māḍhari (*and*) hero of the Ikhākus (Ikshvāku family). The *Āvesani* (mason) Sidhatha (Siddhārtha), a resident of the village Mahakaḍurūra, son of the *Āvesani* Nākachanda (Nāgachandra), a resident of the village Nadanūra in the country of Kamāka, his mother Nāgilini being foremost, and together with (*his*) wife Samudani (Samudriṇī), son Mulasiri (Mūlaśrī), daughter Nākabudhanika (Nāgabudhnikā), brother Budhinaka, (*his brother's*) wife Chakanikā (Cha-kri-ṇikā), sons Nāgasiri (Nāgaśrī) and Chandasiri (Chandraśrī), daughter Sidhathanikā (Siddhārthinikā), also with his caste-fellows, friends and relations, erected in all 5 *Āyaka* pillars at the eastern entrance of the great Chaitya of Bhagavān Buddha in the village of Velagiri. His own charitable gift established for the welfare and happiness of all sentient beings.[4]

The Paṇḍit remarks that as this king Purushadatta is said to be of the Ikshvāku family, he can hardly belong to the Āndhrabhṛitya family who are never called Ikshvākus in their inscriptions hitherto found. "The five pillars that were erected are called *āyaka* (Sansk. *āryaka*) or 'worshipful' pillars, but I have not met with any other instance in which the adjective *āryaka* has been applied to pillars." "The donor Siddhārtha and his father Nāgachandra are called *āvesani*. *Avesana* means a factory or mason's workshop; and one who possesses such is called *āvesanin*. From this I infer that they were head masons or owners of workshops. There is a similar gift by a mason under king Śātakarṇi on the gateway of the Sānchi tope, which I read:—

Rāno Siri Sātakaṇisa
āvesanisa Vāsiṭhiputasa
Ānaṁdasa dānaṁ.[5]

Sanskṛit—

Rājñaḥ Śrī Śātakarner
Āveśanino Vāsishṭhīputrasya
Ānandasya dānam.

"Gift of Ānanda, son of Vāsishṭhī, mason of the illustrious king Śātakarṇi."

---

[1] This follows the lines and generally the reading of the third and most perfect copy.
[2] The *cha* in this name looks very like *e*.
[3] See *ante* p. 27, note 1, and *Ind. Ant.*, vol. x, p. 273.—J.B.
[4] Dr. G. Bühler of Vienna has likewise translated this inscription. His version and remarks will appear in the *Indian Antiquary*.—J.B.
[5] See Cunningham's *Bhilsa Topes*, p. 264, No. 190 ; *conf.* also p. 257, No. 161.—J.B.

In the path round the stūpa, on the west side, was found an image, in *alto rilievo,* of a Buddha, with an inscription under it in characters of about the beginning of the seventh century A.D., of which the following is a transcript and translation by Mr. J. F. Fleet :—

Transcription.

[1] *Svasti Bhadanta-Nāgārjunāchāryyasya*
[2] *śishya(shyō) Jayaprabhāchāryya*[*ḥ**] [| *] *Tach-chhishyēṇa Cha*[*ndra*]-
[3] *prabhēṇa kārāpi....satu Sugata-gata-prasāda-viśēsha-viśishṭa-saṁsārē dēvam=anu*[*chintya*]
[4] *vibhūti-pūrvvakaṁ Buddhatva-prāpti-nimittaṁ Buddha-pratimā pratishṭhāpitā* [| *] *Anumō-danām=ē*[*va*]
[5] *kurvvantu sarvvē Saugaty-ādyē(?)bhyō(?)=pi* ||*

Translation.

Hail! The disciple of the *Bhadanta* Nāgārjunāchārya (*was*) Jayaprabhāchārya. By his disciple, Chandra-prabha, having meditated on god in this worldly existence, which is distinguished by the characteristic of the favor belonging to Sugata,.....................,[1] an image of Buddha was caused to be set up, preceded by (*a display of*) dignity (*or ceremony*), for the purpose of attaining the condition of being a Buddha. Let all people joyfully approve of even the *Saugatyas*, &c.!

---

[1] *Kārāpi... satu.*

AMARĀVATI — Plate VIII

(a) No. 3 (b)

AMARĀVATI

Plate IX

No. 3

(a) (b)

No. 23B

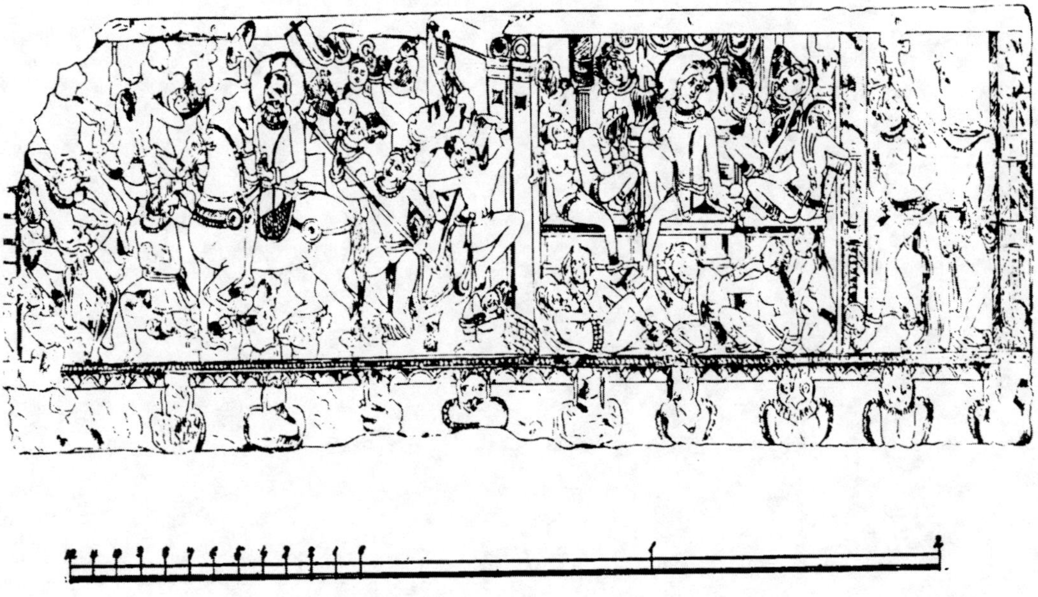

No. 52

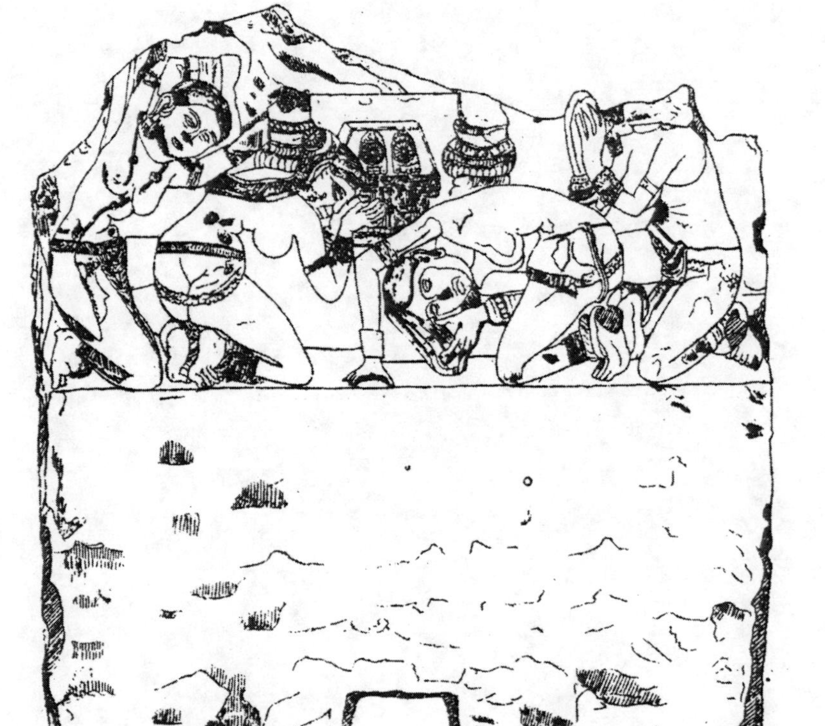

No. 102

(a)

No. 51 B

(b)

No. 44 B

(c)

No. 36 B

(d)

No. 139

AMARĀVATI

No. 206

(a) (b)

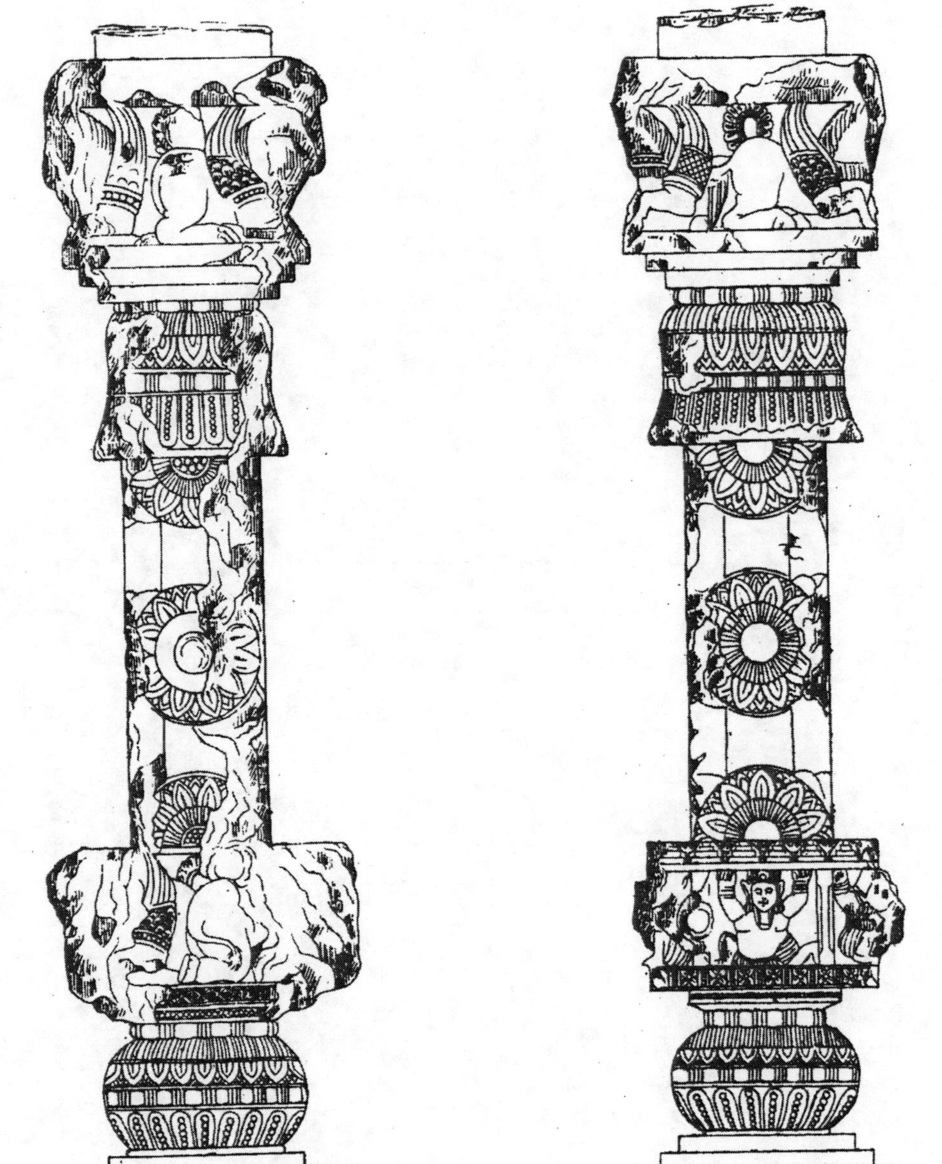

AMARĀVATI

Plate XV

No. 146

(a)

No. 156

(b)

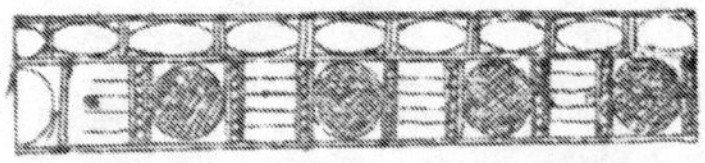

No. 155

(c)

No. 166

(d)

No. 164

(e)

No. 171

(f)

No. 193

(g)

(h)

AMARĀVATI

Plate XVI

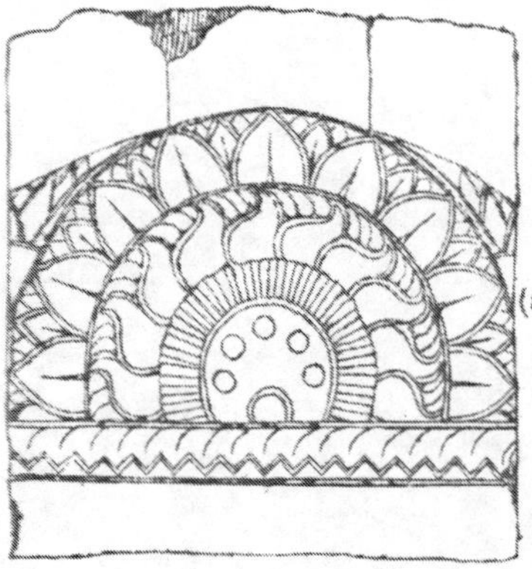

(a)

No. 6

(b)

(c)

No. 20

(d)

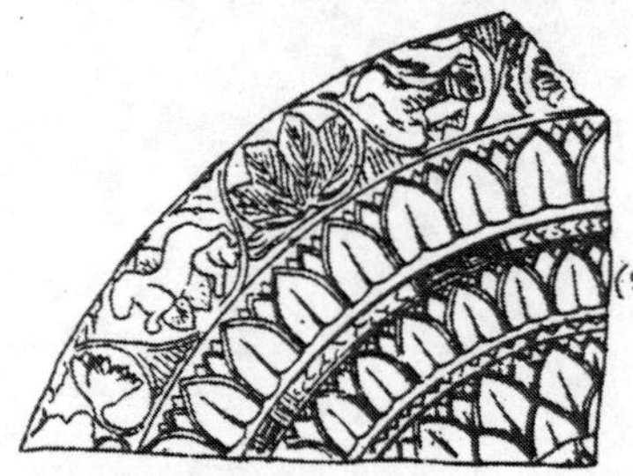

(e)

(f)

(g)

No. 11

(h)

ERRATA.

Page 6, line 4. For *Vaniyasa* read *Vāniyasa*.
„ 6, line 5. For *bheriyasa* read *bhariyasa*.
„ 8. Slab No. 2B. Inscription. For *natukāya* read *natikāya*.
„ 12. Slab No. 11B. Inscription. For *najakāsa* read *nājakāsa*.
„ 22. Slab No. " 43." *For* " 43 " *read* " 43B."
Id. Slab No. 86, line 3 of Inscription. For *sabhātukāsa* read *sabhatukāsa*.
Id. Do. line 4 of Inscription. For *sagharasutāya* read *sagharasunāya*.
Page 25. Slab No. 114, line 2 from bottom. For *samitanāni* read *samitanāti*.
„ 27, line 2 from top. For *dhamachaka* read *dhaṁmachaka*.
„ 35. Slab No. 174, line 1 of Inscription. For *sapi-* read *sapā-*.
„ 43. Slab No. 74B, line 1. *For* " part " *read* " 23 letters."
Id. Do. Inscription. *For* " ? ? " *read* " etc."
Page 44. Slab No. 217. Inscription. For *atavāsikasa* read *atavasikasa*, or perhaps *aṁtivasikasa*.
„ 47. Slab No. 249, line 2. *For* " begins " *read* " reads."
Page 49. No. 88B, line 1. Before " 146 " insert " No."